HEART TENDING

Creating rituals that nurture
you and those you love

KARIN WATSON

"Have you ever been burdened with more "shoulds" than you can handle? Or perhaps, you've been cursed with the need to be perfect in every way. These unresolved conditions can cast a melancholy fog over your angst-filled life. But, if you listen to your heart, all you really want is to be with family and friends, revere what is important to you, and have fun. Karin helps you do that in her book. When you can grasp her concept of ritual, you will see how it can be a liberating force that frees you from yourself while at the same time connecting you to those who are most important to you.

The value of a ritual is its momentum. Ritual has the ability to carry you into a moment of connectedness and wellbeing that adds meaning to your life. Once you've established a successful ritual, then you can use it over and over again to take you where you want to go. If a particular ritual works for you, then you're exactly where you want to be. If not, then a little maintenance is required. You'll know when this is the case because your heart will tell you. So tend to those course corrections as needed, or, if need be, create a new ritual that will capture those feel-good feelings that might have otherwise slipped away. The goal here is to keep the baby while throwing out the bath water. This book has "how-to" insights on ritual creation and wonderful anecdotes that let you feel what others have felt. But you'll want to do more than read the book, participation is a required ingredient."

~Richard Dahl, Father, Grandparent

"Heart Tending is an engaging book and powerful teaching tool filled with practical information, first-person stories, and resources at the end of each chapter. A gentle and inspiring "must-read" for parents and educators."

~Mary Gentry, Parent Educator

Karin shares her thoughts about "heart tending" and ritual through a very personal lens. Her many anecdotes and reflections help us to not only recognize and validate rituals that have been part of our lives for a long time, but new rituals to emerge.

~Kristin Sampson, Teacher and Grandparent

Heart
Tending
Creating Rituals
that Nurture
You and Those
You Love

For Janine
Gratefully for your wisdom
about the parts of my body
needing help -
All the Best
Karin Watson

Karin Watson

For my daughter Kate, her husband Jim, and my son Lee
who continue to be
my best guides and teachers.

For my parents Alvera and Ordin Lein and the Ole Store
whose hard work and attention to seasons
gave me such historical richness for ritual.

For my friends Audrey, Alice, and Winky; their creative force
and clarity helped me when there were no words.

For my former students, who shared their stories and learning.

An elder Cherokee Native American was teaching his grandchildren about life. He said to them, "A fight is going on inside me…it is a terrible fight, and it is between two wolves. One wolf represents fear, anger, greed, arrogance, resentment, pride, and superiority. The other wolf stands for peace, hope, humility, kindness, benevolence, generosity, and compassion. This same fight is going on inside of you and every other person too."

They thought about it for a minute and then one child asked his grandfather, "Which wolf will win?"

The old Cherokee simply replied, "The One I Feed."

Contents

How to
Use
This Book

Ritual connects us to ourselves and to those we love. My intention is to help you make "ritual" a living and vital part of your life by noticing the rituals you already practice, recognizing their power, tweaking them if you see the need, and creating new rituals to fit your changing needs.

This is not a book of "shoulds" or "do mores." You will not find how to throw the perfect birthday party. What you will find here is a way to notice and bring intention to those practices you do and to strengthen connections with those you love.

Within each chapter there will be icons to denote three essential components:

Heart Icon: The definition of ritual the chapter is addressing. Holiday, Family Traditions, Life Cycle and Day-to-Day rituals are the ones we hear most about. I have added a chapter on Repair because I have come to believe it is at the heart of family life, and yet does not get much attention. My hope for the reader is that in thinking about each kind of ritual, they have an opportunity to come to their own understanding of the meaning for themselves and for their own family.

Story Icon: A story to illustrate the value of the ritual. These stories come from my 45 years of working with families in parent education in Community Colleges in Minnesota and Washington State, and at the Island County Health Department. It did not take long into my work with young families that I realized both the joy and the stress rituals bring to family life. The names and settings in the stories are changed a bit to protect those who have so openly shared with me.

Book Icon: Resources for me always come in a variety of sources. The resources I have included are ones that have been shared by my students as well as ones I have discovered. You will find a list of chapter-specific resources at the end of each chapter. You will also find a list of general resources in Chapter 8. The resources in the chapters fall under the following categories:

1. Recommended books for adults and children.
2. A query for discernment, a Quaker practice of sifting through what we have heard or read while listening from an open place in our hearts. There is an answer to a question and the question is answered by outside information. A query is within us to answer. It is called discernment because it is a process that requires ongoing revisiting and monitoring as you grow and as things change in your life. My suggestion is to read the query, write down your own reflections on the query, and then discuss your feelings with other family members or friends. Remembering that you are not looking for one answer but incorporating many answers into a meaningful practice.
3. Quotations to reinforce why a ritual has value.
4. Poetry I have found that captures the essence of the ritual, as well as being inspirational.
5. Music that reminds me of the ritual.

I wish there had been a book like this when my children were young. I struggled with how to create meaningful family rituals in line with my own values. While I tried to ignore the magazine images of the perfect family celebration that showed up in every checkout line for every seasonal celebration, I still felt the need to imitate those magazine pictures.

In trying to make my table look like those pictures, it only created more stress, not the joy and reverence I was hoping for.

I wanted guidance on how to have every member of the family participate in celebrations and not leave all the planning and preparation up to me. I remember how my mother was exhausted at every celebration because she did all the work by herself. I wanted to change that pattern.

It was a struggle early on to know if we were going to celebrate with my husband's family or with my family. Someone always felt left out. When was it time to do our own family event? Whose family tradition do we adopt? How could we be inclusive and not exclusive?

All this pressure left me very emotional. I wanted someone to give me permission to start from scratch. I came across a Cheyenne saying, "Our first teacher is our own heart," and I realized I wanted my own heart to teach me how to ignore the perfect celebrations depicted in the media. Those pictures showed how a celebration should look and paid little attention to how it felt. I wanted my celebrations to be informed with my deepest values. It took time and attention, but I have learned to value the work and the process.

This book is about rituals. I have gone through many titles. When asked what I was writing, I often fumbled with what to call my work. I often found myself saying simply it is a book on how to love one another! That title comes directly from my mother. There were four children in my family of origin and we would be in the living room fighting and my mother would come in from the kitchen, put her hands on her hips and yell, "Love one another!" She would then race back to the kitchen. Needless to say, this response to fighting did not help me learn tools to figure out how to "Love one another." However, her steadfast and enduring love over time gave me clues.

In my 45 years of working with families I have been trying to figure out how to help families do just that: love one another. It is not as easy as it sounds, because we are all so different. I have come to believe that rituals are one tool for sharing love. For me rituals provide tools that first help us to love ourselves by being truthful about what nurtures our own hearts. It is in this process that we become alive and mindful. Then the challenge comes in staying alive in our own hearts and finding a way to come together and connect with others. I emphasize both the process and the work that must be done. It is difficult to put this process into words because it is different for everyone, and it involves asking hard questions.

Rainier Maria Rilke said, "Have patience with everything unresolved in your heart, and try to love the questions themselves as if they were locked rooms or books written in a very foreign language." Taking time to formulate my questions can sometimes be enough. Rilke goes on to say, "Don't search for the answers, which could not be given to you now, because you would not be able to live them. And the point is to live everything. Live the questions now. Perhaps then, someday far in the future, you will gradually, without even noticing it, live your way into the answer." (Nouwen, Henri, *Reaching Out*)

When I ask the questions and allow myself to be patient and curious, the answer surprisingly comes to me when I realize I am living it.

Chapter 1
RITUAL: The Dance of Connection

When I want to tend my knowledge—I go to school.
When I want to tend my mental health—I go to a therapist.
When I want to tend my physical health—I go to the gym.
When I want to tend my heart—I go to ritual.

Anonymous

Heart tending is remembering moments. I remember what heart tending felt like when I was a child: The coziness of Dad's lap after dinner, the relief when Mom put the imaginary monster in the closet before turning off the light, the thrill of Uncle Stan's high-five, and watching fireworks on the Fourth of July. These are moments that I've carried with me long after I passed through childhood.

I want to give the same moments to my children, but the fact is that my life is very different today. Dad comes home late or is out of town too often to count on that cozy lap. I might be too distracted by my phone to notice my child's fear of something that is not tangible. Uncle Stan is living on another continent, so the high fives have become virtual. Though I can't pass on the old ways as I experienced them, I can create new memories for my children that pass on the feelings of belonging, security, predictability, and comfort. These kinds of heart-tending memories are the core of ritual, and they nurture and feed our Spirits today.

As a parent educator, I often ask students in my classes about their family rituals. I believe the first step in ritual is to notice those we already practice and to recognize what they do for us. The most common response I heard was, "We don't really have any rituals." But when I asked what they did around holidays or transition times, such as bedtime, the phrase, "We always..." would repeat itself. "We always go see the fireworks on the Fourth of July"; "We always watch movies on Friday night"; "We always go to Aunt Judy's for Seder"; "We always read a chapter book before bedtime." I then point out that what they are describing is, in fact, ritual. Rituals are what I always do, and I always repeat them because they center my Spirit and provide the glue that helps me connect to others. I am not alone. Rituals are tangible reminders that I belong to a family, a community, and a divine purpose. I count on them, I know they will be repeated, and they are vital to my Spirit.

When I use the word "ritual," some people think of it as some exotic ceremony or the cultural practices that are depicted in National Geographic photos. True, those are rituals, and they certainly tend the hearts of those involved, but a broader understanding of ritual can uncover the potency that ritual holds for me personally. The Oxford Dictionary defines "ritual" as "a religious or solemn ceremony consisting of a series of actions performed according to a prescribed order...regularly done by someone."

In this book, I am using the term "ritual" as a connection. Through ritual, I first connect within myself, and then I connect with those I love. Ritual sometimes involves a prescribed order—sometimes they are tangible, (candles, incense, and water), and sometimes it is about remembering moments like a kiss good-bye. However, the process of a ritual is not as important as the connection one feels when the ritual occurs. The connection provides ways to help us tend our hearts and the hearts of people we love. It gives a sense of security, and it also provides a sense of belonging.

The Hundred Penny Box
Rituals can give children "happy memory banks" that can sustain and nourish them throughout their lives. A mother of two, Julie's favorite bedtime story for her child was *The Hundred Penny Box* by Sharon Bell Mathis. The story sparked an idea for a birthday ritual that memorialized her children's personal histories, providing a box full of memories.

In the book, a great aunt, who is sick, comes to live with her nephew's family. She is one hundred years old and has a box with one hundred pennies in it, one for each year of her life. On days when she is feeling well enough, her grandnephew is allowed to come into her room and pick a penny out of her one-hundred-penny box. She then tells him a story from that year in her life.

Julie now gives her children a penny on their birthdays with that year's date, a card, and they each have a special box to keep them in. She writes something on the card that happened that year in her child's life, something that happened in the family, and something that happened in the world. She then attaches their school picture to it. Sometimes on rainy days, she will find her children in their rooms, pennies all laid out, reading their cards. Julie created a birthday ritual that reminded her children of their personal history, their family history, and how those histories fit into the world. Her children took it one step further; looking at their boxes became a rainy-day ritual as well, and one that nourished their inner lives by being a source of personal history they could return to again and again.

Ritual provides a powerful tool in creating strong families. Whether I recognize it or not, I have family rituals. It might be the ritual of a bedtime story, or pizza every Friday night, or any repeated activity that you do and would miss if you didn't do it. They may seem mundane, just "something I always do." All rituals, however ordinary, are every bit as important as those I read about in *National Geographic* or those I see in a more religious setting, like a church or temple. Ritual is the organic nutrients that enrich the soil of my life, encouraging healthy growth in my Spirit as well as in my relationships. Practiced over time, rituals provide predictability and continuity, two essential ingredients for my sense of security and belonging.

At this point you might be thinking, "I don't need another *should* in my life. When am I going to find the time to plan rituals, for goodness sake?" My hope is that once you notice the rituals you are already doing and notice their benefits, you will gain a perspective about the spirit they bring to you, as well as their power for connection with others. A new perspective might come with this kind of honest reflection.

A favorite quote from the book *Don't Push the River* by Barry Stevens, is "My per-spectacles keep falling off my nose." I know that

4

perspective gets lost when I forget to notice what is really going on when I feel I ought to or should be doing one more thing. This quote was illustrated in a story told by the writer Henri Nouwen. At the time of the story, Nouwen was teaching at Harvard. He was in his office trying to get some work done, but students kept coming in and interrupting him, and he was getting frustrated. He took time to stop for a moment, and in that moment realized that the interruptions were his work. This change in perspective helped him see that student interruptions were the most important work. I heard Nouwen's story when my children were young, and it was an influence on my own parenting. My definition of parenting is that "parenting is one big interruption." When I get frustrated because every moment is interrupted and I cannot get my work done, I remember Nouwen's words. With my per-spectacles back on my nose, I can see that my work *is* the interruptions.

Ritual Objects

When I have taught classes on ritual, I sometimes started by asking each person to bring a ritual object—an object carrying a memory for them—to the next class. It was for me the most meaningful moment in teaching a class. One man brought a wrench his father handed down to him when he bought his first house. Tears rolled down his checks as he shared many moments of being at his father's side as a child handing tools while his father fixed things. This wrench held a connection memory to his father. He now uses the wrench with his own son. One woman brought a wooden spoon that had been well used by her mother. She said she uses it when she makes soups and feels her mother's spirit in the spoon. Another woman brought a silver bracelet that her mother had worn every day and when she was married her mother passed to her. So then when her daughter was married, she felt it was time to pass on this ritual object to her daughter. Another man brought a belt buckle that was his father's and shared how much it meant when before his father died, he had passed it onto him…and humorously reminding him to "wear the pants in the family." Ritual objects hold the power of connection to past and to the future.

My own experience of ritual

I grew up in a family that celebrated many holidays, had many Scandinavian traditions, acknowledged life cycle events, and practiced many day-to-day rituals. Ritual was in everything we did. I knew that my family of origin was different from other families but it was not until I was married that I realized how different we were. When you become a new family you bring with you all the ways rituals were practiced that you never thought about. The challenge then becomes figuring out how this new family is going to perform ritual. It took time and work and lots of uncomfortable questions, and in the end I felt that my children experienced many good memory-making rituals as they grew up, different of course than the ones I grew up with.

When my marriage ended, many of the rituals I believed in and practiced evaporated. Holidays, family traditions, life cycle and day-to day-rituals had to change. Nothing I tried to bring from the past really worked. Someone was always missing. What we "always did" had to change and I knew it. It was not until I could give up my expectations of how things would be that I began to breathe new life into my own rituals.

My first realization was that I needed to move away from the community I lived in. Everywhere I went people asked me how I was doing. I had little privacy for my own grief and I felt I needed to be strong for my children. I also came to know if I was ever going to heal from this, I needed to start over and build a new community for myself. This transition took 14 years of new experiences, work and life style change.

In this process I also became aware that I needed to do something with my wedding ring. It was a symbol of such a sacred trust for me, and it was broken. After much reading and thinking about what I needed, I decided to bury my wedding ring in my new front yard. I knew it was something I could not do by myself. It took courage to ask a circle of friends to help me. We sat on my front porch and talked about what this meant for me, then together dug a hole, buried the ring, and planted a bush. All symbolic of the new life I needed to discover. After we buried the ring we ate and drank and celebrated all the new things I knew I was facing.

This journey, from family life, through divorce and into new beginnings, gave me insight into how families work and don't work. Having to create new rituals to replace the old ones has been a learning experience. I have now come to know and value ritual as always changing to fit the new normal. Mostly, I have come to learn firsthand about the healing power of ritual, and I want to share that with others. This book has allowed me to do just that. Ritual is the mystery guest in our life. We are never sure how to perform it. We certainly know when Spirit is present or when it isn't present in what we do. When Spirit is present we feel a sense of connection. When Spirit is not present we feel a sense of obligation. Ritual is ours to create, change, and share when we find places to do that.

Books for Adults

Rituals for Our Times: Celebrating, Healing, and Changing Our Lives and Our Relationships, by Evan Imber-Black, Ph.D., and Janine Roberts, Ed.D.

This book is the best all-around resource for reflection on ritual. It offers new and inspiring pathways of looking at ourselves, our families, our communities. It helps us tap into the power of ritual to bring vitality and deeper connections to all our relationships.

Only the Heart Knows How to Find Them: Precious Memories for a Faithless Time, by Christopher de Vinck

This book reveals the beauty of the ordinary, the truth hidden in the small event in life.

Books for Children

The Hundred Penny Box, by Sharon Bell Mathis

It is a ritual connection between a boy and his aunt.

What You Know First, by Patricia MacLachlan

It is always difficult to leave the familiar and move to the new. Rituals can be kept alive in our memory and stay with us forever.

Three Questions, by Leo Tolstoy (both child and adult book)

This story asks us to think about three questions. When is the best time to do things? Who is the most important one? What are the right things to do?

Query

Can you identify a ritual you have for yourself? One you have in your family? One you have in your community?

Quotes

"Love is the only emotion that expands intelligence." Anonymous

"The heart of education is education of the heart." Anonymous

"We are not sent into this world to do anything into which we cannot put our heart." John Ruskin

"Rituals draw a circle around a place or event so that we can be more fully awake to the magnitude of the moment." Gertrude Nelson

"My dear children, perhaps you won't understand what I am saying to you...but you will remember it all the same, and will agree with my words sometime. You must know that there is nothing higher and stronger and more wholesome and good for life in the future than some good memory, especially a memory of childhood, of home. People talk to you a good deal about your education, but some good, sacred memory, preserved from childhood, is perhaps, the best education. If a man carries many such memories with him into life, he is safe to the end of his days. And if one has only one good memory left in one's heart, even that may sometimes be the means of saving us." Fyodor Dostoevsky, in *The Brothers Karamazov*

Poetry

"Where I'm From," by George Ella Lyon, in *Reading, Writing and Rising Up*

I am from clothespins,
from Clorox and carbon-tetrachloride,
I am from the dirt under the back porch.
(Black, glistening it tasted like beets.)
I am from the forsythia bush,
the Dutch elm
whose long gone limbs I remember
as if they were my own.
I am from fudge and eyeglasses,
from Imogene and Alafair,
I'm from the know-it-alls
and the pass-it-ons,
from perk up and pipe down.
I'm from He restoreth my soul
with cottonball lamb
and ten verses I can say myself.

I'm from Artemus and Billie's Branch,
fried corn and strong coffee.
From the finger my grandfather lost
to the auger
the eye my father shut to keep his sight.
Under my bed was a dress box
spilling old pictures,

a sift of lost faces
to drift beneath my dreams.
I am from those moments -
snapped before I budded -
leaf-fall from the family tree.

Song

"Wanting Memories" Isaye Barnwell, in *Sweet Honey in the Rock*
I am sitting here wanting
Memories to teach me—
To see the beauty in the world
Through my own eyes. (repeat)

You used to rock me in the cradle of your arms
You said you'd hold me till
the pains of life were gone
You said you'd comfort me in times like these—
And now I need you, and you are gone

I am sitting here wanting...
Since you've gone and left me.
There's been so little beauty—
But I know I saw it clearly through your own eyes

Now the world outside
Is such a cold and bitter place
Here inside I have few things that will console
And when I try to hear your voice
Above the storms of life
Then I remember all the things I was told.

I am sitting here wanting...

I think on the things that made me feel
So wonderful when I was young
I think on the things that made me laugh,
Made me dance, made me sing
I think on the things that made me
Grow into a being full of pride
I think on these things, for they are truth.

I am sitting here wanting…
I thought you were gone,
But now I know you're with me
You are the voice that whispers
All I need to hear

I know a please, a thank you
And a smile will take me far
I know that I am you and
You are me and we are one
I know that who I am
Is numbered in each grain of sand
I know that I've been blessed
Again and over again.

I am sitting here wanting…

Chapter 2
The Barrenness of
Busy Life—
Slow Down the Hurry Up

Socrates was right when he said, "Beware of the barrenness of a busy life." I often hear people say things like, "Life is spinning out of control," "There is no time in my day for reflection," "Every minute is scheduled," and, "I feel like I need to be in two places at the same time." Busyness is the pace of our lives. There are so many things I want to do; a friend of mine calls this an "opportunity crisis."

Lives buzz with piano lessons, yoga, grocery shopping, doctor appointments, birthday parties, and the list goes on. I feel I have to enrich my life with as many opportunities as possible. And aren't busy people "happy" people?

Weareallsobusywithourjampackeddays.

If I look at this gobbledygook and add some spaces between the words, this sentence begins to make sense. Just as when I minimize what I schedule into the day, I begin to protect space.

We are all so busy with our jam-packed days.

Protecting space is not an easy task. Emptiness and barrenness can be felt in the midst of a busy life if space isn't protected. In order to change, I need time and reflection. It may mean cutting from my day's activities something I enjoy in order to create time to just *be* and space to reflect on what activities truly enrich my life, and what activities I may need to let go of.

Engaging in activities with my loved ones, such as watching my child doing sports, is not as satisfying as simply being present with them. Being present with children builds connections and requires space. This might mean watching them doing a sport but making time after the game to talk about how they felt about the game or about their day. Feelings can too easily go unattended in busy schedules.

When I pay full attention to the ordinary moments, they become everything I need and desire. The simplicity of the sound of the rain, my daughter laughing, snuggling under a cozy blanket with a good book, chopping vegetables, the first cup of coffee in the morning…these ordinary moments become extraordinary moments when I simply pay attention.

Perhaps I can learn why busyness leads to barrenness by looking at the ancient Chinese symbol for "busy." Busy has two meanings in Chinese:

Heart Killing　　　　　**Losing one's mind**

In Chinese, the word "busy" is made of two characters—heart and killing—therefore busyness is "heart killing." The Chinese word "busy" is also "losing one's mind." These definitions contradict the American belief that being busy is necessary, stimulating, and fun. However, if I truly tap into how I feel about my busy life, these Chinese translations resonate with me.

In his pamphlet *Tyranny of the Urgent*, Charles E. Hummel writes, "Our greatest danger in life is permitting the urgent to crowd out the important" (pg. 5). When I fully pay attention to the moment or the person I am with, ordinary things like holding hands before a meal, changing a diaper, a bedtime story, or a kiss good-bye, become moments of connection.

Connecting Through an Ordinary Routine

Jim, a father in one of my infant classes, did not like changing the diaper of his firstborn, Peter. He would turn on the television so he could focus on something other than the distasteful task at hand—a poopy diaper. Then Peter waved his little arms and legs at Jim and babbled happily about his freedom. Jim babbled back, and the duet began. Jim turned off the TV and paid close attention to Peter. They cooed, babbled, and made eye contact. Diaper changing became a time when Jim and Peter connected to each other, and they both enjoyed the experience. It became more than just a routine; it became a way to connect.

Listening for Changing Needs

When my daughter Kate was in kindergarten, I would walk her to the bus stop before heading off to work. Kate got used to getting a good-bye kiss. It was her good-luck charm for the day, one that gave her confidence, and a reminder of the security of home. The kiss gave me security too, knowing that Kate was beginning her day with a reminder of how much I loved her.

But I soon learned that children aren't static and sometimes change is needed. I noticed Kate was becoming irritable in the morning, so I asked what was bothering her. Tears rolled down her cheeks.

"I don't want the kiss at the school bus stop anymore. They called me baby, Mom!" Kate wailed. I looked at her trembling lips and big brown eyes and realized that my action embarrassed her. A couple of older girls had teased her, so the kiss was no longer a good-luck charm. As I talked with Kate, I learned she still wanted the kiss, but she wanted it before she left the house.

The morning schedule is a busy time; it would have been easy to be frustrated with Kate's irritability and also to feel hurt that Kate didn't want a kiss from me anymore. By taking the moment to stop, ask, and learn about Kate's dilemma of feeling embarrassed by the kiss but still wanting it, I was able to adjust the ritual while keeping the spirit of the ritual. The new ritual became Kate waiting at the front door, with her lunchbox in hand, to get a kiss from me, then marching off and catching the school bus all by herself.

The routines of these two stories create a space in the busy day. By paying attention to the feeling of connection these everyday spaces provide, being mindful of their impact, and staying open to changing them, it keeps their connection alive and current.

I wish I had a formula for how to slow down. Over coffee, my friend said, "The solution is to just be clear." I went home, looked up "clear" in the dictionary, and found it has thirty-six definitions! Examples: free from darkness, obscurity, or cloudiness; light—bright; shining—free from confusion, uncertainty, or doubt. That is just three of thirty-six definitions. I wish slowing down was easier. It can mean many things but usually involves saying "no." No is a complete sentence. Life becomes more magical when I just slow down and take the time to tune into moments. I can learn more about what my interactions mean and clarify what needs to happen next. This quality goes away when I get too busy; I miss connections that can happen when I pay attention to feelings and am mindful of the present.

Books for Adults

Sabbath: Finding Rest, Renewal, and Delight in Our Busy Lives, by Wayne Muller

Muller calls us to refresh ourselves from the inside out. It can be an hour, a walk in the afternoon, but it is the act of stopping time to refresh ourselves from the inside out. It is time set aside to collect ourselves, to look at our emptiness in the midst of our busy and productive lives. Muller captures the importance of balancing work, family, and rest.

The Hurried Child: Growing Up Too Fast Too Soon, by David Elkind

Elkind calls our attention to the effect of hurrying on children. He offers insights and advice on encouraging healthy development while protecting children.

Books for Children

"Slowly, Slowly, Slowly," said the Sloth, by Eric Carle

Carle celebrates the benefits of slowness and encourages the acceptance of traits natural to us. It illuminates the gift of focus, of child time, and the gifts that come from slowing down.

Query

Where do I find places in my day to stop? How much of my life is on automatic pilot, and how much is mindful? How can I slow down and pay attention to protecting pace?

Quotes

"There is more to life than increasing its speed." Mohandas Gandhi

"To see takes time." Georgia O'Keeffe

"For fast-acting relief, try slowing down." Lily Tomlin

A parent in class said, "Busy: "Where my time, your time, and our time get all mixed up!"

"For children, love equals time—Children spell love T-I -M-E!" Anonymous

Poetry

"A Lazy Thought," by Eve Merriman
> There go the grown-ups
> To the office,
> To the store.
> Subway run,
> Traffic crunch;
> Hurry, scurry,
> Worry, flurry.
>
> No wonder
> Grown-ups
> Don't grow up
> Anymore.
>
> It takes a lot
> of slow
> to grow.

"Yes," by William Stafford
> It could happen anytime, tornado,

earthquake, Armageddon. It could happen.
Or sunshine, love, salvation.

It could, you know. That's why we wake
and look out—no guarantees
in this life.

But some bonuses, like mornings,
like right now, like noon,
like evening.

"Self Improvement Programme" by Judith Viorst, in *Necessary Losses*
I've finished six pillows in Needlepoint,
And I'm reading Jane Austen and Kant,
And I'm up to the pork with black beans in Advanced Chinese
Cooking.
I don't have to struggle to find myself
For I already know what I want.
I want to be healthy and wise and extremely good looking.

I'm learning new glazes in Pottery Class,
And I'm playing new chords in Guitar,
And in Yoga I'm starting to master the lotus position.
I don't have to ponder priorities
For I already know what they are:
To be good-looking, healthy, and wise,
And adored in addition.

I'm improving my serve with a tennis pro,
And I'm practicing verb forms in Greek,
And in Primal Scream Therapy all my frustrations are vented.
I don't have to ask what I'm searching for
Since I already know that I seek

To be good-looking, healthy, and wise,
And adored.
And contented.

I've bloomed in Organic Gardening,
And in Dance I have tightened my thighs,
And in Consciousness Raising there's no one around who can top
Me.
And I'm working all day and I'm working all night
To be good-looking. healthy, and wise.
And adored.
And contented.
And brave.
And well-read.
And a marvelous hostess,
Fantastic in bed,
And bilingual,
Athletic,
Artistic...
Won't someone please stop me?

Songs

"Stop! In the Name of Love!" Sung by The Supremes
    I sing this song to myself in those moments of realizing I am too busy, and I am not paying attention to myself or my children, and/or I am doing things in a mindless way. For me, this also includes eating mindlessly. "Stop! In the Name of Love" has become a good mantra to have tucked away in my own bag of tricks.

"The 59th Street Bridge Song (Feelin' Groovy)," by Paul Simon
Slow down, you're movin' too fast.
Got to make the morning last.

Just kicking down the cobblestones.
Looking for fun and feelin' groovy.
Bada, Bada, Bada, Bada, feelin' groovy

Hello lamppost whatcha knowin'?
I've come to watch your flowers growin'.
Ain't cha got no rhymes for me?
Doot-in' doo-doo, feelin' groovy.

I've got no deeds to do, no promises to keep.
I'm dappled and drowsy and ready to sleep.
Let the morning time drop all its petals on me.
Life, I love you, all is groovy.

Chapter 3
Holidays—Can't Live
With Them,

Can't Live Without Them

Holiday rituals often have great potential for enriching communities and nurturing families. They have a special power because many people in my own cultural or religious group celebrate these days at the same time—days so commonly commemorated they are already marked on my calendar when I buy them. Easter, Passover, Ramadan, Kwanza, Christmas are just some of the days listed on my current calendar. Every year Chase produces a calendar of events for the year. It contains more than ten thousand holidays and while interesting, if I used this as my calendar, I would find myself in a flurry of mandatory celebrations. When I intentionally choose to celebrate just the holidays that resonate inside me, my celebrations began to have more meaning.

We learn to count on holiday rituals from one year to the next, and even from one generation to the next, giving us stability over time. They tether us across time and space to those we love, providing memories that nurture our connection to our inner lives, and give us the resources to deeply connect to those in our current lives.

The Manger

Each Christmas my father built a live manger scene next to the Ole Store, my family's café, grocery store, and meat-locker plant, which was in the small college town of Northfield, Minnesota, where we lived. The manger was complete with straw bales, mannequins dressed like Mary and Joseph, a live bewildered cow or two, several sheep, and a donkey. I remember how I felt as I drove the Ole Store truck out to the farms to collect the animals and straw bales. The farmers' expressions of delight at being able to contribute to the yearly ritual left me with a warm sense of community. It became a ritual to many families. They would stop to visit and feed the animals. Church choirs came to sing carols next to the manger. I loved this tradition, and no wonder! It had all the elements of ritual. I felt included and necessary, inspired by the scene's divine message of love, and I counted on this special connection to family, faith, and community from one year to the next.

With my father's death also went the elaborate Christmas and Thanksgiving displays that were his signature contribution to the family and the community life of Northfield. After becoming a parent of two small children, I had an overwhelming urge one Christmas to set out a manger scene, a crèche set that reminded me of the live one I had helped create next to the Ole Store. Tears rolled down my cheeks as I placed each piece on the coffee table in our new home. Curious, my children asked why I was so sad. I took a moment to share with them the happy and tearful memories the manger scene brought for me. For my children, our conversation was a connection to their grandfather they did not know. For me, it was a reconnection to a treasured holiday ritual.

Yet holidays are not always times of joyous connection to family and community. Many experience the silent demons of stress, anxiety, and even depression during these times that are supposed to be full of holiday cheer. The "holiday blues" affect many people. Right after Thanksgiving until about New Year's, my son-in-law playfully sings, "It's the most horrible time of the year."

In fact, after spending a holiday with extended family, a parent shared with me his tip for getting a reservation at a hotel that is usually booked full every year during the holiday season. He starts calling the hotel on December 26 and calls every day until the first of the year. There are always cancellations during that time, when disappointing family holiday experiences are fresh. The best intentions for family gatherings can result in a miserable vacation, and plans are often changed for the next year.

The spirit-filling potential of a holiday is also easily destroyed by materialism. Financial constraints contribute to holiday stress. Many families spend 95 to 100 percent of their income just paying day-to-day bills and find the holidays an easy time to overspend. I once saw a greeting card depicting a couple. The woman was gazing into her husband's eyes with a conversation bubble that said, "Oh, darling, let's go into debt." Commercialism feeds my desire to please and gives me the empty promise of making everyone happy with just the right gift. Even as I experience the momentary thrill of the purchase, I know I will be dealing with the stress of unpaid bills in January. Yet unpaid bills may be the least of the damage caused by relying primarily on gifts as a focus of the celebration.

Often parents find their children creating elaborate lists of toys, a list that is often influenced primarily by friends and ads seen on television. Instead of spending time with children, many parents find themselves giving in to the powerful force of consumerism. The unintended consequence can be that children learn to gauge their happiness on what they get. Even worse, what gets taught is to value stuff instead of relationships. Shopping for what children want often seems to be the most efficient way to make a happy holiday. When I pause and let myself think for a moment, I know that is not true. The affection and love I want to convey during holiday times happens when I give my children full attention, and take the time to create events that deepen relationships within the family and in my community, that highlight what I truly value.

Memories bring their own unique set of challenges to the holidays. Good memories can stand in my way by keeping me from the flexibility I need to keep the spirit of ritual alive and useful even when everything has changed from my own childhood. One parent shared that she mostly felt mad at her own mother during the Christmas holiday, because when she was a child, her mother made the holidays seem easy and fun. "I don't know how she got everything done; she made it look simple." This mom felt she could never produce a holiday like her own mother did for her without feeling total exhaustion.

For others who have bad memories from childhood, holidays can become filled with a sense of dread; and they become a time to survive, not a time to renew relationships.

Young families can struggle to decide whose family they will celebrate the holiday with. Suggesting that something needs to change signals "you don't love me anymore" kinds of reactions. Trying to please both sides of the family works for a while, but celebrating holidays with both families, rushing from one home to others to celebrate, just as I used to do, can make the celebration a burden rather than a ritual that is nurturing.

Rituals need to change over the years. In fact, when rituals are rigidly adhered to despite the changes going on in family, the ritual will become a negative force. In the movie, *Fiddler on the Roof*, Tevye, the main character, has to learn how to adapt to change (what to keep and what not to keep). When someone has entered or left the family, the rituals need to change to reflect this shift. Finding a balanced approach to celebrating takes time and lots of talking. Most parents find that asking children to dress up, to be nice, to smile, and to display perfect manners all in one day does not work. Something needs to change.

Young children live in the world of *now*, not in the world of the future, even though the future may be just a few hours or days away. So instead of rushing to meet everyone else's expectations or our own unrealistic schedule of activities, take a deep breath and slow down to consider the words of Mr. Rogers in his book, *Talk With Parents,* about making holidays special for children. Do things that:

- are familiar and traditional (an example is making luminaries together—candles in bags to be put out to line a walk at night and to welcome guests);
- are done before the holiday itself (together baking and freezing);
- are done together (everyone cooks together and has a part in meal preparation);
- have personal association—an expression of your own values;

- reflect the real inner needs of children (this changes at every developmental stage);
- don't cost much money (taking a walk with your child and looking at lights).

Jesse Jackson once said, "Your children need your presence not your presents." That is the beauty of holiday time. It is a time of being together and doing things together that create memories that sustain and nurture. I owe it to my children to slow down, to nip and tuck, and tailor rituals to fit my children's needs. In that way, I model what is really important during holiday times: to be in a relationship with the ones I love.

Many families today struggle with what I call the three D's: death, divorce, and distance. Often these bring feelings of grief and loneliness. Because of this, our holiday time requires a special kind of reconnaissance duty. Since they are steeped in tradition and culture, it's easy to get stuck in a rut and continue year after year without stopping to examine the tradition's usefulness. When a holiday celebration brings a sense of "Why am I doing this?" it is no longer a satisfying ritual and it is time to ask myself, "Does this celebration connect me to Spirit? Does it enhance my connections to others? Is it carrying my intended values?"

Changing and Keeping Spirit of Ritual Alive

Dan, a father, talked wistfully about the Christmases he experienced as a child. The weekend after Thanksgiving, Dan and his family picked out the tree, brought it home, and decorated it. Then his mother taped newspaper over an archway behind where the Christmas tree stood. That was the last Dan saw of the tree until Christmas morning. All he knew of the taped-off alcove during the intervening days was what he heard—his mom or dad's footsteps, the rustle of paper, the thud of boxes—sounds that fed his imagination. On Christmas morning, he and his brothers rushed downstairs only to be stopped at the bottom. There they waited until their dad gave the signal that meant they could burst forth, break through the paper, and open the gifts. The butterflies in his stomach still return when he thinks of it. He not only remembers this Christmas ritual, he still feels it!

Dan hadn't really thought about suggesting this ritual to his wife, Sue, since their current home didn't have an archway, and there was no way to replicate it. When Dan was describing it to the parenting class one evening, he realized that he did not want to replicate the actual event; he wanted his kids, Jack and Sydney, to experience the curiosity, anticipation, and excitement that he remembered. Furthermore, he could only imagine that his parents must have had their own delightful times creating their secret cache of packages. Dan and Sue began to brainstorm their own ritual. So around the first week in December, boxes without names appear behind the couch, inside the cupboards and closets, in the garage, the basement, the utility shed, the attic, and anywhere else they can think to put them. Not until Christmas morning do Jack and Sydney get their treasure-hunt directions so they can locate their gifts. The buzz now is not what's behind the archway, but where are the boxes, and who do they belong to? Eventually, Jack and Sydney decided to get in on the fun and create a treasure hunt for their parents.

The essence of ritual is Spirit. In this case, all it took was the realization that a ritual is not a rigid event based on the belief that "it's tradition" and there's only one way to do it right. Dan was able to pass on the spirit of his beloved Christmas ritual when he recognized the essence of it: was curiosity, anticipation, and excitement. Dan and Sue adapted the ritual to fit their new circumstances. The change allowed the spirit of this ritual to continue for their children.

"Blood, sweat, and dinner" is the way too many families celebrate Thanksgiving. There can be too much emphasis on the food and not enough emphasis on reason for this holiday. I remember one Thanksgiving dinner I prepared as a young mother and full-time teacher. I was trying to recreate the only Thanksgiving celebration I knew—an old-fashioned sumptuous dinner. I wanted my children to contribute, so I had them make turkey name cards out of pinecones one year. After grace and a reading of the Thanksgiving story, we were ready to pass the food. I looked down and found ants crawling all over the table. The unintended guests were brought in with the pinecones. But as is often the case when things don't go as expected, people adjusted, and a toast to the ants followed.

Humor, compromise, and creativity are what it takes to successfully merge holiday ritual. One mother dealt with her husband's death by setting a place at the table for him during holidays. Then they began the meal by sharing stories about him. Another woman shared with me that after her husband divorced and left the family, every time the family ate together, it would end up in a fight. The table now had three people, and the empty chair reminded them their father/husband was missing at the table. They decided to remove the chair so their missing person was less in their face. Whatever helps a family transition to the new normal becomes the most important thing to do. Sometimes by simply acknowledging the hole, a new connection is made.

Stepping Up to Be a Part

Greg's memory of holidays were of his parents drinking and fighting, the same way they spent every other day. He could not understand why people made such a big deal over holidays. Understandably, he shied away from ritual. Joanie, his wife, loved all holidays and with her enthusiasm and artistic flair, she created interesting activities for their two daughters. Greg felt inadequate during these times and floated into the background. Though Joanie often asked for help, Greg would say that he was too busy, and "just didn't have time for that kinda stuff." Joanie communicated with Greg the frustration and disappointment she felt when he declined. Greg also realized that he was beginning to envy all the fun they were having. This was enough for Greg to start thinking about a family activity he could initiate.

One Halloween Greg suggested to his daughters to help him shop for pumpkins to decorate their front step. The ritual of pumpkin carving began and grew as the girls grew. Pretty soon they were roasting pumpkin seeds and making pumpkin pie, as well as carving pumpkins. One year his youngest daughter wanted to make whipped cream for the pumpkin pie, but they didn't have a mixer. By this time Greg was well into the spirit of ritual making and suggested that they put the cream in a jar, place the jar in a coffee can with a bit of padding, and roll it back and forth like a soccer ball. Now, they have a mixer and can whip the cream into a nice, firm Martha Stewart creation, but they still choose to roll their cream in a jar each Halloween. They celebrate their connection to each other, with an activity they are pretty sure is unique to their four-some. If the ritual continues into the next generation or two, someone will be sure to ask, "Why do we put up with this wimpy whipped cream? Why don't we use the mixer?" That will be the time for passing on a great family story. It may even be the time the family decides to make an adaptation and use the mixer, carrying the spirit of the remembered ritual into the new.

Acknowledging where each of us uniquely comes from allows us to accept the reality of what *is*, and gets us to the next step, which is to navigate the shift. What do we do now? Every family has challenges. Communicating is key to creating a holiday that is not sidetracked by resentments but is inclusive of the traditions that are important to each person. The transition from past to present can be guided by asking the central question, "Now that things have changed, how can we keep what is important to each of us?" Once family members acknowledge the change that has occurred in their lives, they will be better able to let the past stay in the past and enjoy the present. But not everything has to change. Talking with children about what they want to keep may be what keeps the "spirit" of the holiday alive for them. Adults also need to pay attention to exactly what puts "spirit" into their holiday. Once each person shares what he or she wants to keep or change in the holiday celebration, the challenge may be how to fit it all together.

Distance

"Absence makes the heart grow fonder" is a truism that comes into sharp focus during the holiday times when we are separated from family and friends. Rituals that acknowledge our wish to be together during these times of separation will ease the loneliness and communicate the essence of connectedness we experienced in the past. One parent told of a Valentine card her children sent to their Uncle Tom who was in Iraq on military duty. The children decided to trace their hands on construction paper and attach them to paper arms long enough to wrap around Tom's chest. This strong, muscled, tattooed young man was curious when he opened the envelope with the long-armed hands that stretched very far, and it made him smile. He taped them to his bunk, and they remained a daily reminder of a couple of kids back home who loved him.

A friend who traveled widely in her career as an international educator developed a ritual that eased her loneliness at holiday times. The week before Thanksgiving, she said, "I held an open house." There was always a homemade, flat, foil-covered box shaped like a turkey with many holes in it for candles. The ritual began when the lights dimmed, a big tray of wine and juice was passed around, and each person gave a toast to those they would miss the most during the holiday. Amid many tears and much laughter, the guests shared their emotions and were heartened by the ritual.

One of my favorite Halloween stories came from a mom who had a twelve-year-old and a four-year-old boy. It was Halloween and the four-year-old had the measles and could not go out to trick-or-treat. His older brother had an idea. He closed each bedroom door, then he took his brother by the hand and they knocked on each door for a treat. When the four-year-old came downstairs, he was all smiles. He had his bag of candy! Sometimes the most memorable holidays are the ones that ask us to improvise the most.

Jackie remembers one Christmas when she was nine years old; her father had taken the entire family to Germany for Christmas. He had business there and didn't want to be separated from them. As Christmas neared, Jackie began to think more and more about the Christmas holiday she was missing back at the farm with her grandparents. She managed to stay a bit interested in sightseeing, but the hotel room was small for the family of five, and though there were Christmas decorations in public places, nothing festive greeted them when they returned to their tiny hotel room.

Then Jackie's mom had an idea. "Maybe we can find a tree branch and decorate it." And for decorations, she said, "Well, I've never seen so many pretty candy wrappers. We can just eat our candy and save our wrappers. By Christmas we'll have a decorated tree."

The Power of Symbols

For Jackie, the Christmas tree was a symbol that gave concrete expression to the festivity of the season and her grandmother's central role in it. She missed the tree. She missed her grandmother. Without her grandparents, Christmas felt lonely. Jackie's mother wisely realized that though she couldn't bring Jackie's grandparents to Germany, she and the family could create a Christmas-tree experience that evoked for Jackie her grandmother's festive ritual.

As Jackie's story vividly shows, we bring personal meaning to the symbols we use in ritual. Children don't automatically find meaning in symbols and neither do adults. In Jackie's case, the tree was all about those happy times she spent with her grandmother decorating the tree. Our experiences with symbols determine their meaning. A Christmas tree may not mean much to a child whose mother wants such perfection that she decorates it by herself or she brings the local florist in to do the job. The experience is lost, because participation is the key. When children listen to stories, light the candles, say the prayer, and sing the songs, they are taking in the meaning of symbols with which they are working. The richness of symbol can be found in a private family story known by everyone such as "we always make *lefse* at Christmas because it reminds us that all Grandma and Grandpa had were potatoes those first Christmases they were in this country." Though the story may be well known to the adults in the family, it is important to tell the children the story so they, too, can understand the significance of *lefse* as a symbol of their family's humble beginnings and a reminder to appreciate the struggles of ancestors who "made do" with what they had. For children and adults alike, making *lefse* becomes a celebration of a family story that transmits a family value.

Symbols tap into our shared human history on many levels—national, religious, ethnic, etc. Children grow in their appreciation of a symbol as they learn the stories and histories associated with it. Creating the Kwanzaa display of candles, corn, the unity cup, and other Kwanzaa symbols with parents who relate the meaning of each piece, builds the foundation with which children can begin to take in the universal significance of the ritual, as well as begin to understand their own family's commitment to building strong families and communities. Likewise, learning the history of the Christmas tree helps children realize that we share a human history, as well as a religious history, when we decorate a Christmas tree. An illumined tree first appeared centuries ago, celebrating the winter solstice, lighting up a dark time of the year, and reminding people that there were sunnier days ahead. As a Christmas symbol, the tree has gone through many changes—from symbolizing the solstice, to the illumination of Christ's birth, to the light that we intentionally bring to the world. Symbols are powerful because they tap into our shared human history, a history that is often beyond our consciousness. When choosing symbols for our rituals, we can choose from an array of vehicles that will carry our values and have the power to bridge time and distance to illuminate spiritual and interpersonal truths.

A holiday is not simply about the here and now; its essence lies in a family's cultural and religious story that has been passed forward through generations. It is here that we can be intentional and choose the values that we want to pass on to our children. If we take time to reflect on what we think is important about the holiday, we can create rituals that are personal and have the vitality to inspire.

The ABCs of Cultivating Holiday Rituals

A—Acknowledge what is going on. Sometimes it takes a while to sort out what is going on during a holiday time. Sitting down and taking the time to *talk about it* together may be as important as finding a *solution*.

B—Brainstorm about what might help. What comes from listening to each person's perception, including each child, no matter the age, may surprise you. It may give you clues as to what needs to stay and what you can let go.

     C—Cultivate the resources, the people, and the participation. Having the courage to make changes may require uncomfortable transitions. Gather support from as many sources as you can.

     This chapter is the longest chapter in the book. For years, I heard the anxiety rise in parents about holidays beginning around Halloween. One year I heard a definition of leadership: Leadership is a calm presence in an emotional field. It takes courageous leadership to stay calm, and we owe it to ourselves and our children to find way to create celebrations that protect our Spirits in the highly emotional field of holidays.

Books for Adults

Unplug the Christmas Machine, by Joe Robinson and Jean Coppock Stacheli

This book is dated, 1991, but it is filled with many creative ways to think about holidays and sort out family values. It helps identify the things around a holiday that matter most in your family.

Books for Children

The Secret of Saying Thanks, by Douglas Wood

This presents a larger and more powerful message about the meaning of giving thanks.

Family Read

Miracle on 34th Street, by Valentine Davies

A good one-chapter-a-night kind of book.

Query

What gives you Spirit for the holiday you are celebrating?

Bring to mind a problem you feel incapable of solving during the holiday. What is the first step you take? How might you develop a shared vision in a current challenge?

This is an exercise I gave students after a holiday to fill out and tuck away, in order to remember the kind of planning you might want to think about for the next holiday.

Reflecting Back on a Holiday—Looking Back to Plan Forward
Remembering the past, reflecting on the present, redoing the future
- What was your favorite moment this holiday? What was your least favorite?
- What do you think was your child's favorite moment?
- What did you learn about the importance of rest?
- What did you learn about food?
- What were the biggest stressors?
- This is what I want to remember for next year...

Quote

"Tradition is a guide not a jailer." W. Somerset Maugham

"Childhood feelings are the oldest footnotes in you. The child in me is the foundation of my life. I go there in all my writings. It's about imaging, imagination. Two days before Christmas my brother died. So Christmas got all mixed up with Sunday, Easter, Good Friday and all the clocks broke in my mind. All the Seasonal boundaries broke." Herb Brokering

"If you truly hold a stone, you can feel the mountain it came from." Mark Nepo

"We are connected by the things we do together. There is regularity, a consistency to what we do as a family. Quite simply: rhythm and ritual are what we aim for; predictability may be what we can achieve." Kim John Payne

Poetry

"Kid Stuff," by Frank Horne (written in December, 1942)

> The wise guys
> tell me
> that Christmas
> is kid stuff...
> Maybe they've got
> something there
>
> Two thousand years ago
> three wise guys
> chased a star,
> across a continent
> to
> bring
> frankincense and myrrh
> to a kid
> born in a manger,
> with an idea in his head...
>
> And as the bombs
> crash
> all over the world
> today
> the real wise guys
> know
> that we've all
> got to go chasing stars
> again
> in the hope that we can get back
> some of that

Kid Stuff
born two thousand years ago.

"Artists," by Judy Edenstrom
Record the color of their lives
On paper wet with water.
Colors running out of control
Like our minds
Like our lives.

Play like three year olds
Splashing color like toys or
Candy sprinklers

Joy in the accidental
Combinations like
Ukrainian Sushi and
Japanese Borscht
For American English Teachers
And German Grad Students.

"Holidays" by Henry Wadsworth Longfellow
The holiest of all holidays are those
Kept by ourselves in silence and apart;
The secret anniversaries of the heart,
When the full river of feeling overflows;—
The happy days unclouded to their close;
The sudden joys that out of darkness start
As flames from ashes; swift desires that dart
Like swallows singing down each wind that blows!
White as the gleam of a receding sail,
White as a cloud that floats and fades in air,

White as the whitest lily on a stream,
These tender memories are;—a fairy tale
Of some enchanted land we know not where
But lovely as a landscape in a dream.

Song

"Anthem," by Leonard Cohen
Ring the bells that still can ring.
Forget your perfect offering.
There is a crack in everything.
That's how the light gets in.

Chapter 4
Family Rituals…All in the Family

As much as we gripe about Dad's disgusting cigar smoke, make fun of crazy Aunt Sarah, or are downright irritated by Aunt Bessie's critical eye, we need our families. Jan Howard once wrote, "Call it a clan, call it a network, call it a tribe, call it a family. Whatever you call it, whoever you are, you need one." The "mother-father-children" family unit of the past has morphed into a variety of compositions. A definition that better fits today's family is a circle of people who love us—a circle that we are usually, but not always, connected to from birth until death. Babies and children need this circle for physical survival, and if we are to thrive emotionally, spiritually, and socially, we all need a circle of people who love us—teens and adults, as well as babies and children. Our family is our anchoring place, and without it we can feel dangerously uprooted, unsafe, lost, and unhappy. When we develop rituals to celebrate birthdays, anniversaries, and other family events, we are scheduling times to stop and create a space to reconnect with those most important to us whether they are "blood" family or not.

In *Practicing Our Faith,* Sharon Daloz Parks writes in the chapter "Household Economics," "Home is where we let down and rest well—or fitfully. Home is where we figure out primary patterns of nurture and productivity, habits of need and desire, forms of rage and forgiveness, ways of 'taking time' and discovering the people who 'count' for us. Our households are anchoring places where, over time we craft the practices by which we prosper or fail to prosper" (pg. 43). Family rituals give us a way to nurture and to deepen these 'anchoring places.' Family rituals differ from other rituals in that they are dates that only appear on the calendars of family members. When we celebrate birthdays and births, anniversaries, marriages, and adoptions, we acknowledge our joy for the lives of those in our family. When we gather around family rituals, they remind us that we are not alone. We have a place at the table. We are a part of something bigger than just us. When children leave home for college, start a first job, or join the military, these rituals remind us that our family ties remain in place even during times of separation and change.

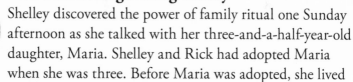 "We were a Burger King Family"

Shelley discovered the power of family ritual one Sunday afternoon as she talked with her three-and-a-half-year-old daughter, Maria. Shelley and Rick had adopted Maria when she was three. Before Maria was adopted, she lived with her mother and her brother in a car. Maria was cooperative and happy from day one, except for Sundays. On Sundays, Maria would waken with her usual sunny disposition, but when it came time to get ready for church, Maria would fuss and refuse to get dressed. She attended Sunday school when her parents attended the service, and her teacher reported that she would bite other children, refuse to sit still, and scribble all over the table instead of coloring on her paper. During the week at daycare, there were no such reports of misbehavior. After church, Shelley, Rick, Maria, and her two older brothers would stop at McDonald's for lunch. Even there, Maria squirmed, fussed, and pestered her brothers. It wasn't the Sunday lunch the family had enjoyed before Maria's arrival. This went on for a long time. Though Shelly and Rick disciplined Maria, nothing changed. Instead of getting used to their Sunday-morning routine and growing out of the bad behavior, Maria's behavior only got worse.

One Sunday afternoon, when Maria had been living with them for over six months, Shelly sat down with Maria to discuss her "Sunday Disposition," as she and Rick had begun to call it.

"Honey, I noticed that when we get ready to go to church, you don't want to get dressed for it. Is there something wrong?"

Maria's lip trembled, and she looked at the floor, shook her head, and muttered, "No."

"Mrs. Clark said you bit Kevin again today and wandered around the room kicking things when the rest of the class was in the story circle," Shelly said. "By the time we got to McDonald's, you were really out of sorts."

When Shelly said the word "McDonald's," tears ran down Maria's cheeks and she sobbed, "We were a Burger King family."

Confused, Shelly murmured, "A Burger King family?" *What the heck does that mean?* "Sweetie, what do you mean, Burger King family?"

"Mommy, we used to go to Burger King every Sunday when I lived with my brother and my other mom."

That afternoon, Maria had provided Shelly with another piece of the puzzle of her life before the adoption. Maria said that most of what the family ate came from dumpsters, but on Sundays, Maria's mom would scrounge up enough money to go to Burger King. It was a ritual that Maria had learned to count on when so much in her life was unpredictable. It was breaking some internal rule to go to McDonald's.

Now the family goes to Burger King on Sundays. Shelly reports that within a couple of weeks, as Maria began to count on Burger King again, her "Sunday Disposition" disappeared.

Maria's words, "We were a Burger King family," was a statement of family identity; it was Maria's way of belonging to a family. The Sunday ritual was so deeply imprinted on her young life that once it was reinstated, she was able to bridge the chasm between her old family and new family.

Rituals shape family identity, deepen relationships, impart values, acknowledge growth, and encourage responsibility. This story illustrates how much power rituals hold in our lives.

Shaping Family Identity

There can be a variety of things families always do that can in fact become ritual. It might be a saying, or it might be an event that gets repeated every season. It may not make sense at first glance. Yet when it occurs, everyone in the family knows what to say or expects to do.

The Watson family sends their children off to play with friends by saying, "Don't have any fun."

The Strom family sends their children to school with "Have a rotten day!"

The Hussey family always sings their own version of "The Itsy Bitsy Spider" at family birthday parties:

"The itsy bitsy spider crawled up the birthday cake.
Itsy quickly learned that he'd made a great mistake.
He climbed up the candle before the cake got cut.
So the itsy bitsy spider burned his little butt."

The Seward family plays hooky from school and work the first day of spring and the first day of winter. In the spring, they might plan a hike to the mountains to see the spring flowers peeking out of the snow. In the winter, they'll find an indoor activity, such as a morning at the curling rink where they taught their children a game they used to play when they were young.

A friend shared something his mother always said whenever he would leave her: "Bless your heart." It has been years since his mother died, but whenever he hears the message, you can see emotion in his eyes!

Family rituals weave a pattern of connection to the family and over time that weaving of shared experience and shared meaning becomes integral with family identity; some call it a "family signature." Families go through many developmental changes, but this ritual connection remains a constant from one stage to another. These signatures have value and give a sense of belonging to every family member. The humor, storytelling, and the repetition are elements that provide family a shared connection. Some writers refer to family ritual as the glue that holds a family together. It becomes a way of communicating intimacy and love and security.

Whatever the shared connection, it is the repeated pattern that gives us a sense of stability and deepens our relationship to one another. This kind of connection builds resiliency. Steven and Sybil Wolin in their book *The Resilient Self* write about growing up with ritual and contend that if you grow up in a family with strong rituals you're more likely to be resilient as an adult. Even in families that struggle with many kinds of adversity, the sense of stability given by rituals can keep the family connected.

Strengthening "I-ness": A Sense of Personal Identity

As parents, we cannot give our children self-esteem, but we can create conditions that will enhance and strengthen their sense of self. What can we do to strengthen a child's sense of themselves, their sense of I-ness? How is that child different from other children? Rituals that celebrate the unique temperament, personality, talents, and heritage of each family member have the potential to create a lasting impact.

Birthdays

Birthdays are a once-a-year chance to give someone a strong confirmation of his or her place in the family. We all have a longing to hear someone say, "I'm glad you were born; I'm so glad you're in my life." It is a very different kind of longing than the longing for material possessions, which can too often become the focus of birthdays. Our lives are "rich" when we know we are part of a family who cares that we are around and that we are doing well every day.

Years ago, I worked as a social worker. Two of my clients, age seven and eight, asked if I would help them plan a birthday celebration for their mother. Though they wanted to buy their mother an expensive gift, they knew it was out of the question since family finances were stretched thin. Instead of buying gifts, they decided to make a book for their mother. The girls drew pictures of all the things their mother did that they appreciated. There were pictures of their mother reading *Charlotte's Web* to them, of their mother waiting for the bus that would take her to work, and another of her cooking chili for their evening meal. They bound the book and put a picture of their mother on the cover that they had taken with a borrowed Polaroid camera. Then they made a big white layer cake and decorated it with plastic flowers. Their final effort was a banner made with butcher paper. The banner read, "Best Momma Ever!"

Their mother's face lit up with surprise and delight as she paged through the book. Tears glistened at the edge of her eyes. For a mom struggling with too little time and too little money, a book depicting her children's appreciation for her hard work in providing a loving family life was the most precious gift she could have received. Feeling recognized for the contributions one brings to family is a deeply emotional experience; it brings tears to even the most stoic of us. When ritual celebrations recognize our individuality, whether it is the role we play in our families, or some unique talent or interest, they bind us to those who have taken the time to notice in deep and eternal ways.

Celebrating birthdays helps us to find a way to mark growth and highlight the changes that come with each year. One family I know marked each child's height on a doorframe every year. When the family moved, they removed the doorframe and brought this valuable marker of growth to their new house. One family, who moved often, marked each birthday's growth on something they called the "grow pole" so they could easily move it with them.

The Carlson family found a unique way to acknowledge their children's growth. They gave their children two envelopes on every birthday. One envelope was marked "New Privilege," and the other was marked "New Responsibility." Age-appropriate privileges and responsibilities remind parents, as well as children, that privileges come with responsibilities.

Birthday celebrations were important in the Edison family. The children celebrated twice—once with the family and once with school friends. Brad's sixteenth birthday was coming up, and Carol, his mother, wondered how to keep a group of sixteen-year-olds entertained for an evening. As was her habit, she consulted with Brad, who said he wanted to invite his friends to Game Gallery. Carol's first response was, "Whew, that's easy." All she had to do was call Game Gallery and let them know the date, time, and number of people. Game Gallery would take care of the games and the food and the price tag was not an issue, so why not? But it seemed almost too easy, and Carol was concerned that a party at Game Gallery was not exactly in line with their family values.

In the past, the children hosted parties at their home, which highlighted interaction with each other, or trips to the zoo that involved learning about the animals; the family value of broadening one's learning or developing relationships had always been a prominent part of the celebration with friends. Then Carol thought of a way to broaden the experience: she suggested that the invitation request batteries for the local homeless shelter, Tent City, rather than gifts for Brad. That way, Brad would not have to write thank-you notes. Brad enthusiastically agreed. On the way back from Game Gallery, Brad and his friends delivered the batteries to the shelter. In this way, a simple birthday celebration became a moment to build awareness of a community need.

Another mother gave her children a hardbound book each birthday that passed along her values of reading and history. She placed their school picture inside the cover and then wrote a letter describing the highlights of the year, taking care to mention family events, school experiences, and friends. Her children, now in their twenties, have a personal history tucked into their library and a great collection of books that continues to grow, as this ritual is as treasured in their adulthood as when they were children.

Staying Connected Over Time

Though family reunions are not as common as they once were, they are even more important in today's world given the distances separating many grandparents, parents, siblings, aunts, uncles, and cousins. Mary Pipher writes about what we are missing in her book, *In the Shelter of Each Other.* "Reunions reconnect the family to extended family and to the natural world and disconnect them from the corporate, generic world. Compared to computer time, everything happens in slow motion. Families talk about who looks like whom, who walks like whom, who talks like whom and who thinks like whom. They compare cobbler recipes and discuss the best way to toilet train toddlers. They tell embarrassing stories about the adults present. This is familial cement. It helps everyone stick together." (pg. 243)

The value of reunions is that the family lore continues to evolve. The stories of ancestors document their struggles, their triumphs, and the current stories of activities and adventures each generation offers. It is the stories that are kept and retold that are important, whether in the midst of a family reunion or in the midst of a gathered circle of friends.

Family stories are great opportunities for strengthening I-ness, "this is who I am," especially when they highlight a unique or admirable trait. This is who I am in this family story.

A Learning Story…I am Courageous, I Can Do

Sue, a six-year-old, went on a ski holiday with her family. She didn't want to be left behind on the beginners' hill, so she gamely tagged along with her nine- and eleven year-old brothers to the intermediate hill. By the third day, she was visibly tired, but she still tugged on her snowsuit and ski boots. Judy, her mom, tried to dissuade her, promising to go to the beginners' hill with her instead. Sue insisted that she wanted to go with her brothers just as she had the two previous days. Judy agreed but told her, "You can go, but if you get too cold or tired, come on back to the ski condo. Promise?" Four hours later when Sue and her brothers returned for lunch, Judy asked her, "My goodness, how did you manage to keep up with the boys all morning?"

"I just plucked up my courage more," Sue replied.

Over the years the story has been told time and again, feeding and encouraging Sue's "can-do" approach to life. Family stories are mirrors for children, telling them what we have seen in their lives, what is worth repeating, and thereby reinforcing their sense of self.

Unique Gifts

Children, like gifts, come in all shapes and sizes. We find them endlessly fascinating when we open up to their unique qualities such as an emotional, intellectual, or physical talent or need, an ethnic background, or a passion or interest that seems come "out of the blue." Yet, when there's more than one child in the family, it's easy to overlook the "special" quality in any one of them in our effort to be fair and efficient. Or sometimes we over-acknowledge the special talents or needs of one child at the expense of our other children whose talents or needs don't seem quite so amazing or challenging. Whatever the case, children can guide us toward the right balance. Picking up on their cues can help us choose rituals that will strengthen each child's sense of I-ness.

I remember a dialogue that occurred one St. Patrick's Day in our car on the way to a friend's house for a party. In the car was my husband, myself, our first born biological daughter (age 8) and our adopted Korean son (age 5).

Kate: Isn't today St. Patrick's Day?

Bruce: Yes, that's why I wore this great, green-flowered tie.

Kate: Oh, yuck! It looks like something you should have left behind in the sixties.

Bruce: Well, thanks, Kate, I'll try to remember to wear it more often.

Kate: How much Irish am I?

Karin: I'm not exactly sure from the Watson/Winsor side, but from the Lien/Seim side you're exactly 100 percent half-Norwegian.

Kate: Yo, Dad, how much Irish are you?

Bruce: Well, let's see, Grandpa Watson was Scottish and English, and Grandma Winsor was Welsh, Scottish, and Irish, so you'd be less Irish than Scottish and more Irish than English or Welsh.

Lee: How much Irish am I?

Bruce: Well, you're 100 percent Korean like your mom is 100 percent Norwegian, but since you're adopted into our family, you'd be Korean, Norwegian, English, Scottish Welsh, and Irish. Wow, that's a lot!

Silence…

Lee: Well, if that's true, wouldn't that make all of you part Korean?

Bruce: Well, yes, I guess that's right. Because you are in our family that makes all of us part Korean. I never thought about it, but you're exactly right!

Kate: Well, I'm not part Korean.

Bruce: Maybe not now, but someday you'll see that another way.

That year I added a ritual. I always placed a Norwegian flag on our table for Syttende Mai each year. I also began placing a Korean flag on the dinner table to celebrate Solnal, the day Koreans celebrate the beginning of the lunar calendar. This simple gesture sent a simple message to the entire family that the family's Korean heritage was also a part of our family heritage.

Celebrating arrival days nurtures adopted children. Some families celebrate on the day a child arrived in their family highlighting the "new family" that was created on that day. Others celebrate their new ethnic heritage by serving ethnic foods for holiday meals. However it is done, recognizing and celebrating adoptions year after year can be a powerful way to celebrate a child's membership in the family.

Family Vacations

One of the statements that was popular a few years back was, "It's called a trip when you take your child; it's a vacation when you don't." Another view of vacation is that it gives one a chance to look backward and forward, and to have time to reset our own inner compass. However, when children enter the family, vacation can turn into a nightmare if expectations are not evaluated ahead of time.

Young families often confuse vacation with visiting family. It is good to be clear that visiting family is visiting family, and it does not always provide the breathing space that vacation time addresses. Just like all family rituals, it is important to have all family members weigh in on what they are expecting with the vacation and this time together. Variations on the vacation theme include physical invigoration, replenishing the soul, entertainment, education, culture, adventure, escape, togetherness, rest, and relaxation.

A new variation on vacation is called "staycation." This is when you stay home but pretend you are on vacation. Perhaps a vacation can be some or all of the above; perhaps one year a vacation is about physical invigoration and the next year it is about resting, and the next year you just stay home and explore your own community.

It is good for adults to keep some things in mind:

- Begin with the right attitude and perspective.
- Remember what the goal is for this vacation and be prepared for what it means.
- Plan on being on duty and entertaining and resourceful even more than usual.
- Plan on pacing and plan on dolling out surprise treats all the way.
- Begin the trip rested.
- Call ahead to see what can be borrowed.
- Remind folks you visit about child proofing.
- Don't expect anything beyond the behavior you see at home.
- Remember there are places in the world where the motto "Children are to be seen and not heard" is still in place.

One vacation I flew with my two children and my mother to Newfoundland where my oldest brother and his family lived. I left the bag of tricks I had to entertain the children at the Toronto airport and all I had in my bag was a roll of masking tape. We taped our fingers together. We taped our mouths shut. We taped our hands to the armrest. I learned from this experience that most of the time I brought too much stuff, and what my children wanted most was to have me present with them and just have fun.

Anniversaries

One of my favorite Ole and Lena jokes is about the couple celebrating their fiftieth anniversary. Lena wakes up in the morning and says to Ole, "You never tell me that you love me, Ole." His response: "Lena, the day I married you I told you I loved you, and if I change my mind, I'll let you know."

Anniversaries are not only for the couple to celebrate. Children are great observers. They watch how we as adults show our love and caring. Anniversaries celebrate partnership. How they get marked and celebrated can be healthy relationship modeling for children. Marking anniversaries in a public way confirms to children that love continues over time.

Family rituals give our children a family identity, a unique community that can strengthen their sense of self, and provide them with a secure sense of who they can count on, who can raise their spirits, who will support them when life is challenging, and who will be there to celebrate their growth events. Family rituals provide a sense of belonging for each member, they build resiliency, and with luck and planning, create good memories.

Books for Adults

Putting Family First: Successful Strategies for Reclaiming Family Life in a Hurry-Up World, by William J. Doherty, PhD.

This work helps us think about the roles our children play in our lives, and the roles we play in their lives. It includes some perspective on how to restore a sense of fulfillment, fun, and security.

In the Shelter of Each Other: Rebuilding Our Families, by Mary Pipher, PhD
This book is about family life and the realities families face.

Books for Children

The High Rise Glorious Skittle Skat Roarious Sky Pie Angel Food Cake, by Nancy Willard
This story is about a young girl who needs to make a cake and uses her grandmother's secret recipe.

All the Places to Love, by Patricia MacLachlan
A very moving story about one family's connection to the land. The child sees all the places to love.

Stand Tall, Molly Lou Melon, by Patty Lovell
A story of a grandmother's words taken to heart by her grandchild, Molly Lou Melon.

Two Mrs. Gibsons, by Toyomi Igus
This is a very heartwarming story about family and heritage.

Query

In what ways do we create a sense of belonging for every member of our family? How do we understand and appreciate each person's contribution?

How do we practice the feeling that everyone has a place of belonging at our table?

What family traditions do I hope will continue to be passed along?

Quotes

"Rituals are part of the glue that holds a family together, a way of communicating intimacy and love and security. They define us as a culture, as a family, as individuals, they change as we change." Nancy Rubin

"People are returning to family rituals because the world is losing a sense of what's important, offering instead shallow beliefs and sound-bite values. Family rituals help people affirm what their beliefs really are." Dr. Roberts

"Celebrations make beginnings, endings, comings and goings, without it we feel emptiness and alienation in our lives." Bepko and Krestan

"The Lord made us family. Miles can't keep us apart. Time can't make us forget. Troubles can't put away our hope and our pride. We go on praying. We go on dreaming. We go on living with peace and courage in our hearts. And we make this world a better home for all generations to come." Ruby Jackson

"To be happy at home is the ultimate result of all ambition." Samuel Johnson

Poetry

"Generations (for the forests of Ellsworth Creek)," by Eve M. Tai
Silence drips,
Hush,
Rain,
Forest, Green cathedral,

800 year old trees
Stand
Next to me,
40 years old.

What lessons do you have for me?
I ask the trees.
They respond:
Your life is what you see above ground,
But underneath,

Where you can't see,
Is what you cannot do without,
for those are the roots of generations.

Song

"There was Music" (as sung by Ronnie Gilbert)
There was music in my mother's house.
There was music all around.
There was music in my mother's house,
And my heart still feels full with the sound

Chapter 5
Finding Support in Our Communities—Changing the Me to We

Life-cycle rituals support my individual growth as I go through developmental changes and begin to adjust to what the new life stage is asking of me. It is a transition time where there are joys, as well as challenges, and the support of a caring community can help with both. The challenge for me in this transition is to identify what new kind of support fits what I now need. It can take time and it can sometimes be informed by support that is not helpful. After my needs are identified, the next challenge is to find a community that can give me support. If I am lucky, support comes from my own existing family, but it may be that I have to create a whole new community for myself. Getting the right kind of support is crucial.

Liminal Time

When I go through this kind of transition, the words "liminal time" best describes where I am. It is a time where the movement of stepping from a present state to a future state is not all figured out. Examples of these times are becoming a parent, baptisms or naming ceremonies, the first day of school, the passage from adolescent to adult, a first driver's license, graduation, wedding, retirement, and funerals. These events represent a shifting time for a person. It is valuable for communities to take note because a new kind of support is needed during life-cycle transitions. A woman has a baby and her sister becomes an aunt, her brother becomes an uncle, and their mother and father become grandparents. The mother of a new baby needs support, which helps her bridge to the new life cycle of motherhood.

Life-cycle rituals point to some big change in life. It is because of that change that we invite the community around us to be a part. Some cultures have very prescribed rituals for each of these events. One such ceremony is the Bar Mitzvah, which is built into the Jewish religious tradition. It signals to the community that the boy is becoming a man. It celebrates the transition in a public ceremony, as well as provides support for the young man beyond the public ceremony.

Owning What You Need

I remember my first few weeks with my daughter, Kate, after we had come home from the hospital. I was feeling very alone. I had just moved back to my home state of Minnesota after being away for graduate school, and I had lost touch with many of my good friends. I was a thirty-seven-year-old new parent. My friends had their children earlier and had all gone back to work.

The woman who lived next door would be out early in the morning hanging her baby's diapers on the line. I would hear her singing as she did her task for the day. In my mind, she seemed an unlikely person to ask for support. (I did not hang diapers out to dry and if I did, I would certainly not be singing.) The days seemed long, and although I loved being a parent, I felt like something was missing. I realized that what I missed most was time to myself to get out for a run. I finally had the courage to ask my neighbor if we could do an exchange—I would watch her child so she could get out, and she would watch my child so I could get the exercise I missed. I learned from this experience that in my transition to parenthood I could ask for help from people I did not necessarily have everything in common with. They did not need to be my best friend, but I knew she would take good care of my child. The experience of asking helped me to identify the new kind support that I was missing.

Another part of this life-cycle transition occurred when I asked to have my daughter baptized. The most surprising and overwhelming part of the service was the "I will" of the sponsors, and the "We will" of the congregation. These simple, resounding words were powerful reminders that a commitment of support for me came from sponsors and from the entire congregation. I no longer felt alone in this parenting journey. The service signaled to the community that I was on a threshold, that I was taking my first steps into mothering, that a new kind of support was necessary, and I needed them in a new way. And I learned that what I needed was to have the courage to ask for support in these new places.

A village can be a family, friends, a neighborhood, a school or a church community, and many other places and people. These community "villages" can be counted on to protect us through the life-cycle changes. In my years as a parent educator, I heard too many parents say in one form or another, "Yes, I know it takes a village to raise a child, but I feel like I am the only person home in the village." In a culture that values individualism, needing others is not encouraged. I think this is most exemplified in a quote from my brother who said, "I do not want it written on my gravestone, 'Here lies the body of a person who never bothered anyone.'" Too often in our culture, we take great pride in never having to bother someone. I go at it alone. Whatever I call this support, mentoring, protective factor, or bothering, the truth is *I need it*! I cannot journey through life without "it." The "it" may be different for everyone, but it's obvious I do not go through life without support. I may have difficulty asking for it and finding it, but there is no denying that I need it.

Eda LeShan, a new mother, stated, "What I kept saying those first months was…'I just haven't got it!' My husband kept asking me what 'it' was and I couldn't tell him. Then my mother decided to come for a visit…When she hugged and kissed me, I turned to my husband and said, 'This is what it was, I needed some mothering myself.'"

I learned about asking for help in a new place when my daughter was in fifth grade. I lived in an area where many children were having Bat or Bar Mitzvahs. I wanted to create some kind of event to help my daughter feel supported as she transitioned to her beginning stage of becoming a woman. I saw a sign in my local community center from Planned Parenthood advertising a class called, "Growing Up Female." I felt this might be the ticket I was looking for, but I did not want to do it outside of a home setting. I called Planned Parenthood and asked if they would ever do this program in a home setting if I did the organizing for the participants. They agreed and I invited ten of my daughter's friends and their mothers for the evening.

The event began with the mothers sitting in chairs in a circle and the girls sitting in the middle of the circle on the floor. The facilitator asked the mothers to talk about their first menstrual cycle and what their mothers talked about with them and how they felt about their experience. Then the facilitator told the girls to sit in the chairs and the mothers to sit on the floor in the middle of the room. They then asked the girls what they heard their mothers saying.

"It sounds like your mother was embarrassed."

"You seem like you don't want to talk about this."

"It is hard for you to say the words *vagina* and *penis*."

All of these responses rang true in the mothers' ears. Next, one of the facilitators took the girls to the family room and showed them a video on what the first doctor's visit might be like. The other facilitator stayed with the mothers and asked them to think about what they could do to create a different experience for their daughters from their own personal experience. This discussion was of great value for me because it gave me some ideas for when my daughter began her cycle.

I had given some thought as to what I would have liked from my mother and was ready. When my daughter began her cycle, I bought her a ring with a woman's face on it at our favorite local gift store. Then just the two of us went out for dinner, and even though she was not particularly thrilled about beginning her period, she was happy with the ring and I felt connected to her. I was grateful for the kind of intentional planning that came out of this evening with moms.

A few months later, my daughter was at school and had forgotten maxi pads, but she felt comfortable going to one of the mothers who was at the Planned Parenthood event to ask for some money (that she would pay back) in order to purchase pads. So my daughter's community of support was broadened by the experience of the evening with friends and mothers.

About five years later, I had a hysterectomy. After surgery, my daughter came along with my husband to pick me up from the hospital. On the dashboard was a gift-wrapped box. When I opened it, I looked into the face of the woman on Kate's ring. It was identical to the one I had given her. She had purchased the ring with her allowance money to honor the ending of my menstruation cycle. It was a full circle gift for me.

The Final Life Cycle

Death is the last of life cycles. We are a culture that for the most part does not talk openly about death; it is an uncomfortable topic to be avoided. Elizabeth Kubler-Ross has helped our culture get over the denial of death and move this final transition stage of life from a "me" to a "we." Her five stages of grief are useful tools to help people identify and face the emotions around death: denial, anger, bargaining, depression, and finally, acceptance. It offers the opportunity for conversation and honest sharing.

A friend of mine shared a very touching ritual that her father did each year. On her mother's birthday, her father would bring her a dozen roses. He had never missed a year in the sixty years they had been together. Her father had cancer and knew he would not be around for the next birthday. He gave his daughter money and a card and asked if she could buy her mother a dozen roses when her birthday came around. Her father knew it would be a difficult time for his wife and had written in the card that he knew he would not be there for this birthday, but he was there in Spirit from wherever he was. This surprising continued ritual brought great comfort to her mother and the daughter, and it was because the father had the courage to talk about it before his death.

When working primarily with young families, I experienced the sadness of many miscarriages. What is often said to women is some version of, "Try not to feel bad, you are young and can try again." I struggled finding ways to give support to the devastating feelings around such an experience. I found this piece written by a mother and it helped me to give a message of support.

"No need to Mourn," by Jan Harcourt
Some would say that you weren't
really a baby, that there is no need to mourn.
But for hours, weeks, months
my body felt you—the promise of new life.
In my dreams I saw you—asleep in my arms.
And, alive with hope, my heart began to love you
a mother's love: fierce, gentle, like no other.
Some would say that you weren't really a baby.
And it's true; there are no photographs, no first smile, no name.
Not even a birthday,
just a date when grief comes due each year.
Some would say that you weren't really a baby,
that there is no need to mourn.
But I mourn you.
The grief rushes in to fill my hollow body
and I mourn the broken promise, the dreams unfulfilled,
the loss of love.

A favorite grandmother in my former neighborhood was asked by her grandchild about death. The grandmother had been sick, and the child observed her not being able to do some of the things she had always done. Her grandchild was filled with anxiety and told her one day that she did not want her to die. Her response to the child was immediate and went something like this: "You know, honey, when I die, I will be closer to you than I ever was here on earth because I will be in your heart!" What a wonderful reassurance to a young, anxious child. The grandmother's honesty helped her grandchild see death in a whole new way.

In life-cycle rituals, we move into a new geography. When community is in place to help me map out this new terrain, I do better. The security that comes from being supported helps us to feel loved and accepted at the very core. Whether it is a community of one or many, we do better when we do not go through transitions alone; the life of "quiet desperation" disappears in the face of support. Every person must define what "it" is, and "it" will be different for every individual. It takes some intentional creating. Healthy growth comes out of such experience. We are not alone; we discover again just how much we need a village when we pay attention to life-cycle ritual.

Books for Adults

From Beginning to End: The Rituals of Our Lives, by Robert Fulghum

This explores the rituals that mark the natural passages of human life. He helps us think about the "holy" rather than the "how-to" of rituals.

When There are No Words: Finding Your Way to Cope With Loss and Grief, by Charlie Walton

We all have times when no words seem appropriate. This well-written book helps find an understanding that loss is part of life.

Books for Children

Wherever You Are: My Love Will Find You, by Nancy Tillman

A wonderful reminder that love is the best gift we give children and they can carry that with them every day of their lives.

Lifetimes: The Beautiful Way to Explain Death to Children, by Bryan Mellonie and Robert Ingpen.

This is a very simple but honest way to begin to talk about death with a young child.

Yay, You! by Sandra Boynton

Moving out, moving up, and moving on! There are so many choices. The world is immense. Take a good look around and decide what makes sense.

Throw Your Tooth on the Roof (Tooth Traditions from Around the World), by Selby B. Beeler

Teeth fall out every day, all over the world. What do you do with yours?

Query

Recall a time in your life where you felt real support in a life transition. Was the support in the form of a person, place, or thing?

Quote

"The heart has its own memory. Each friend represents a world in us and it is by this world that a new world is born." Anais

"It isn't the changes that do you in, it's the transitions." William Bridges

"Nothing we do, however virtuous, can be accomplished alone; therefore, we are saved by love." Reinhold Niebuhr

"Perhaps this is the most important thing for me to take back from beach-living; simply the memory that each cycle of the tide is valid, each cycle of the wave is valid, each cycle of a relationship is valid." Ann Morrow Lindbergh

Poetry

"Closing the Circle" by Wendell Berry

Within the circle of our lives
We dance the circles of the years,
The circles of the seasons,
The circle of our reasons
Within the cycle of the moon.

Again, again we come and go,
changed, changing. Hands
join, unjoin in love and fear,
grief and joy. The circles turn,
each giving into each, into all.
Only music keeps us here,
each by all the others held.
In the hold of hands and eyes
We turn in pairs, that joining
Joining each to all again.

And then we turn aside, alone,
out of the sunlight gone
into the darker circles of return.

Song

"Circle of the Sun," by Sally Rogers
Babies are born in a circle of the sun
Circle of sun on their birthday day (repeat)

Clouds to the north, clouds to the south
Wind and rain to the east and the west
But babies are born in a circle of the sun
Circle of the sun on their birthing day.

Other verses

Children take their first step in a circle of the sun
Children speak their first word
I hope to be married in a circle
And I hope to die

Chapter 6
What We Do Every Day Counts Big Time:
Routine or Ritual

Day-to-day rituals are the most practiced rituals in our lives. They can also be one of the most overlooked. Their repetition makes them seem almost automatic, like a routine. However, there is an emotional difference between routine and ritual. A routine, like making my bed or brushing my teeth, might be repeated over and over, but if it does not happen on a given day or at a given time, life can still go on fairly smoothly. The way to recognize the value of ritual as opposed to routine is to have it interrupted or not happen for some reason. *Watch out!* If a daily routine has become a daily ritual and it does not happen, there is something not right about the day; something feels missing. It is the F.O.M.O. (Fear Of Missing Out) factor at the deepest level in our Spirit.

This missing something is the emotional connection that ritual brings to our lives. These very small daily practices may seem like ordinary moments, but for me they carry with them a place to touch down with the source of life, to brighten my Spirit, and to keep me going. These moments can carry a deep richness of connection and comfort to my life. They contribute to the feeling of wellbeing by serving as organizers for the day; they bring predictability, consistency, and most importantly, they provide a spirit of feeling grounded. I can trust in myself and I can trust in the world.

The day-to-day practice of ritual is the seedbed that cultivates over time a healthy memory bank, and the best collection I can give myself and my children is this: a healthy memory bank. Memories live inside me. They do not bind me to the past but instead remind me that I can survive no matter what shows up. Life brings times of joy, times when I feel loved and cared for, and also times when I just simply survive a hard, emotional period. Memories filled with this kind of vitality honor all the experiences life brings. Having negotiated the demands of the past, I can walk with confidence into the future. I can have faith that I will survive and flourish.

Dad's State of the Union Address

I remember my father, Ordin, beginning each day quietly sitting in his chair in the lamp-lit corner of the living room with a cup of coffee and notepad in hand. I remember teasing him that he could not begin his day without fueling up on "Norwegian gasoline!" He would answer quickly with a twinkle in his eye, "Just doing my morning State of the Union address." Little did I realize how much this ritual meant to him until I found some of those notepads after his death. By reading through the notepads, I found out that this time of day was more than just drinking a cup of coffee; it was the beginning of his daily ritual. The notepads were filled with to-do lists, some sort of doodling, and they always included something he was thankful for, as well as something he was worried about. It was a surprise for me to read that his thankful list usually included something he was proud of that one of his four children had done, and it was not a surprise that his worry list was usually around paying bills. This ritual gave my father a predictable and meaningful rhythm to his life and it grounded his day. This very ordinary time carried him into a deep connection to himself, his work, and his faith.

Years later I realized I was repeating this ritual modeled by my father. I remembered the notebooks I found as I drank my morning coffee and made my own lists for the day. I recognized my father's inspirational modeling of his everyday "leap of faith," his powerful belief that things would work out if you just show up and keep doing the work. Over the years, this day-to-day ritual has become a framework for me as well; it sets a tone for my day and makes me feel more connected to my work, my Creator, my father, and most importantly, to my Spirit.

What Lives in our Adult Memory Banks?

One of the ways to access your own early memory bank is to think about sensory memories as a child. When I ask students to do this, the lists always turn out very poetic. Take a moment to make up your own list.

Smell
- What do you remember smelling as a child?
- "Smell is a potent wizard that transports us across thousands of miles and all the years we have lived." Helen Keller
- Examples: Dad's aftershave, lilac bush in bloom, yeast bread rising, Vicks VapoRub, moth balls, morning coffee, cinnamon, grandmother's perfume, attic smell, wet dog

Seeing
- What do you remember seeing as a child?
- "Nobody sees a flower—really—it is so small it takes time—we haven't time—and to see takes time, like to have a friend takes time." Georgia O'Keeffe
- Examples: Lights at Christmas, balloons at parties, fireworks, leaves changing color, crocus, rainbows, photographs, the Northern Lights, full moon, cookies cooling, zoo

Hearing
- What do you remember hearing as a child?
- "Music, the perfume of hearing." Diane Ackerman
- Examples: Rain, thunder, blackbirds, trains, cuckoo clock, wind, fire whistle at noon, fog horn, radio shows, tea kettle, the Mitch Miller Band, laughter, "Ho, ho, ho," rooster

Tasting
- What do you remember tasting as a child?

- "If an event is meant to matter emotionally, symbolically, or mystically, food will be close at hand to sanctify and bind it." Diane Ackerman
- Example: Tomato fresh from garden, camping food, S'mores, sweet corn, trees, ripened orange, fried smelt, gingerbread, Pepto-Bismol, egg nog, saltwater, bacon, olives

Touching
- What do you remember touching as a child?
- "Touch, by clarifying and adding to the shorthand of the eyes, teaches us that we live in a three dimensional world." Diane Ackerman
- Examples: Bone-dry Grandpa's hand, sand in bathing suit, slippery oil cloth on table, smoothness of baby's bottom, Grandmother's hugs, Dad's scratchy face in morning

When I begin to reflect on my own childhood memories, I notice that what comes to mind rarely involves a monetary value or some elaborate prop. The value of thinking about sensory memory is that it puts me in touch again with very ordinary moments and invites me to a basic reconnection to myself and the world around me.

A common memory for adults is music, usually a lullaby. A powerful quote by Henry Ward Beecher says, "What a parent sings to the cradle goes all the way to the coffin." Music connects those synapses in our brains. If you want to teach your child their phone number, put it to music and they will learn it quickly. Think about the power of the ABC song. People who work in the hospice field often share how much music means to the dying person, and it usually is a song that was a part of their early development.

Our first place to learn about day-to-day ritual is in our childhood home. It is learned by having a predictable everyday pattern; what we always do. It is where we discover the people who will stick by us in all our fits and starts of becoming. The world is very chaotic when we first emerge after nine months in a very protected and safe place, the womb. Consistent routines help build our security in this new world. These routines include being fed when hungry, changed when necessary, comforted for sleep, and stimulated enough so brain neurons can grow. This begins the learning that life is predictable, the world is safe, we have people to count on, our basic needs are met, and, most important, we can now tend to our own discovery and exploration our own rituals.

Transitional Times

Transitional times are not just for children but are a part of life at every age. They include transitions from sleeping to waking, from being hungry to being fed, from work and school to home, and finally from bedtime to sleep. Parents often complain they just get used to what is needed for their child and then a transition is necessary because things have changed developmentally, and this new geography demands a new routine or a new connection. The yin-yang ancient Taoist symbol of life depicts this kind of change. One state gives birth to another state. In William Bridges' research, he calls transitions, "getting through the wilderness." He specializes in finding resources for organizations in transition. He writes, "It's not the change that is hard; it is the transitions." These in-between times can be challenging because they demand a shift for us, whether it is in the workplace or in our day-to-day personal transition times. When I pay attention to what is demanded in those shifting times, I can seek out resources that help me find ways through the transition time and the wilderness. By doing this kind of reflection, I begin to feel more connected to myself and to those who care about me.

During times of transitions, there is a natural tendency to develop a new kind of routine or ritual. A friend shared that when she went back to work after having children, she would come home and put her keys in a drawer by the back door, then immediately wash her hands. It became a way for her to transition from work to home. She realized that after her first year back to work, this routine had become a ritual. Putting the keys in a safe place represented the ability to begin a new day without hunting for them. Washing her hands helped her feel like she was washing away the cares of work. This ritual helped her connect to herself, and to separate work and home so she could become more present to herself and her family. It was a transitional routine and now if it is interrupted she finds that she has to go back and redo coming home. It has become a day-to-day ritual. Something is not quite right if it does not happen.

It takes intentional thought to turn routine into ritual. Ritual is a very individual process as well as a developmental process. The kind of needs at each transition vary for everyone individually and at various developmental stages. I remember that I wanted home to be a safe environment for practicing and learning all manner of things. In paying close attention to what is needed day to day in times of transition, a powerful contribution to a healthy memory bank is made.

Morning Rituals

In the children's book *The Way to Begin the Day*, Byrd Bayor talks about an elaborate ceremony to begin the day for a child. It begins by seeing the blessings that come from all directions—north, south, east, and west. Although it reflects a wonderful Native American ritual to the start of a day, our modern pace usually does not permit time for such a lengthy ceremony. However, we all do develop some kind of daily round. We discover times in the day that bring meaning and grace.

Contrast waking to an alarm clock verses waking to the sound of footsteps bringing you tea every morning before school, a ritual one friend's mother did every day for her through middle and high school. Friends have shared that their morning greeting went something like this, "I want to hear feet on the floor, now!" Another morning greeting on a more humorous note, "Get out of bed, we need the sheets for a tablecloth."

Love Dad is a collection of notes Patrick Connolly wrote to his boys every morning because he left for work before his kids got up. The book is described as: "A father's daily epistles to his two boys...written on the run and left on the breakfast table." This book is a happy and insightful experience to read and a wonderful reminder to "take time." This simple daily ritual gave his sons some inspiring words of advice, support, and encouragement to face their day.

How do you create a pattern for meeting your world each morning? Opening the curtains, letting in the weather, turning off the alarm clock, unlocking the door, getting the paper, getting dressed, making the bed, having your morning coffee…these morning patterns may just be routines for you, or they may contain an emotional connection that helps to enrich life and create a predictable order for the start of the day ahead.

Returning Home Rituals

The hour at the end of the day, when family members are returning from work and school, is sometimes known as "Hurricane Hour." Everyone is a bit tired and hungry. It can become a time of emotional upheaval in family life. Routines at this time may help but developing some individual rituals help this hour go more smoothly and have the possibility of changing hurricane hour into happy hour.

Ideas:

One dad shared that he would stop on his way home from work and have a cup of coffee and read a paper. This gave him some breathing space between work and home. When he arrived home, he would be better prepared to be present to his family.

A mom shared that she would listen to classical music on the radio. The music nurtured her Spirit and helped her transition from work to home.

Having a light lunch ready for children when they return from school helped one parent nurture her children. Too often parents bombard children with questions about their day. It is not surprising that children rarely want to talk about their day the minute they come home. We forget that children need separation time just as adults do.

Ending the Day Ritual

Bedtime represents the last transition of the day. How do we say good-bye to our day?

Since predictability is the hallmark of ritual, it is important to establish a clear bedtime sequence, at least through school age. Bath time, teeth time, story time, whatever the order, it becomes a time of connecting. What helps us feel connected to ourselves and family may make a huge impact on how sleep goes.

Ideas:

One family developed a Greats and Grumble book. The book was beside their child's bed, and the last thing of the day was for a child to identify something great that happened that day and the parent would write it in the book. Then, the child would identify a grumble, and that would be written down as well. It was a way for their child to think about their day but also a way to instill the notion that life is full of all kinds of things, and no matter what, you will survive both the greats and grumbles. What a treasure for an adult to read over and reflect on their childhood.

A mother shared that her son was having a lot of worries that would show up before bedtime. He had a favorite teddy bear, and this mom made up a ritual on the spot. She had her son tell the teddy bear what he was worrying about so he could go to sleep and the teddy bear would stay up all night worrying. In the morning, the teddy bear and her son would have breakfast together, and then he would tuck the teddy bear back in bed so he could sleep and her son would take over the worries. It was an on-the-spot ritual that helped get a child over a difficult spell in his life. There are now Guatemalan Worry Dolls that have been passed down as a way to share your worries so you can sleep. This may be a good idea for adults as well as children.

Playing a music box each night was one family's way to end the day with their child. They played the same song every night.

Years ago I made up what I called "tuck me in" cards. Each card had an idea. At bedtime, a child can select a card, and it becomes a way to have a conversation with a child to end their day. Examples: Name some happy words, tasty words, scary words; I'll make an animal sound and you guess what I am; Tell me a story about when you were little; What are you looking forward to tomorrow?

No matter how we do them, these patterns of our day become fixed patterns without anyone really thinking about them. I lived next to a family that had a set of twins. On my way to work each day I would drive by them as they were walking to school. I would always stop, roll down my window, and say, "Have a rotten day."

One day, their mother came over to say they would be moving. She had asked the twins what they would miss about the neighborhood, and what they reported was quite a surprise to her. They said unanimously that they would miss the daily exchange they had with me. So when they moved, I sent them postcards with the words, "Have a rotten year." Their mother told me that those postcards stayed on their individual bulletin boards all year. You never know when a set of words become a ritual! They are more than words, because they provide continuity and a way to transition through our days.

Eat Together—Eat Better

There was a movie made in 1987 called *Babette's Feast*. It is the story of a person who went to great lengths to prepare a meal for a family torn apart by petty squabbling. As the family begins to eat together, the conversation begins, and soon old turfs between people soften. Pouring hours into food preparation may be one message of this. The fast-food nation may see something from this message. However, I feel that the movie's more important message is that when we eat together, conversation follows. It is important to note that the realistic part of the film is that this complicated and precise food preparation only happened once. Making a meal does not need to be elaborate.

Eating is not just a matter of fueling our bodies but also a matter of fueling and strengthening our connections with each other. Eating together becomes a communion that helps us remember that we need each other, that someone cares how our day is going, that we get checked in on. When we eat alone or in front of a TV, those kinds of connections are lost.

Eating three meals together *is* an impossible task for modern-day families. However, routinely having Sunday morning breakfast, Friday night pizza, or Tuesday night dessert together can be an opportunity for today's family to create a ritual around eating together that accomplishes the kind of check-ins that are important.

Childhood obesity is on the rise. We do know that our eating habits growing up have lifelong effects on our eating habits as adults. Paying attention to what we eat and how we commune will create long-term healthy nutrition.

Some Ideas Shared From Families

We light a candle when we sit down to eat, whether it is breakfast, dessert, a meal, or a snack. It signals a beginning of eating together. The fun for the children is getting old enough to light the candle and of course blowing out the candle at the end of our eating time. Taking turns is a learned side benefit.

We always have Friday night pizza, and all family members can invite a friend to share this dinner with our family. As the children get older it becomes a time to eat together and then to run to the Friday night events. It allows us to have a quick weekly check-in time, and it expands our family and provides a time to get to know our children's friends better.

Lunch-box notes were the way I stayed connected when my children were in school. By middle school, my children did not want me sending notes in their lunch box, but in cleaning out their rooms years later, I found that both children had saved all those lunch-box notes.

The Windsor family had individual napkins and plates for each member of their family. They sat at the same place every time they ate together, and each person who set the table knew which seat belonged to each member. Mrs. Windsor often left surprise notes under one person's plate. It usually contained a question that could be discussed as a family during the meal.

The Howard family said that their family had invited a friend of their five-year-old and her mother to an impromptu dinner after a play date. As they sat down to eat, the kids requested to start the meal with the family chant. Their child reached out to hold her friend's hand, but she was hesitant and looked for her mother's approval. Her friend said in a loud, determined voice, "Mom, I am not praying!" The Howard family had to giggle and assure her that the chant would not be a prayer. It was a German rhyme taught to them by their grandma. "*Piep, piep, piep*, we like each other very much. Everyone should eat as much as they can, except the person next to them." This is finished by rude, caveman-like fists banging on the table and the command, "Eat now." The Howard family loves it and are always proud to show off this family tradition to visitors.

Another family shared that they hold hands and say, "We have our bread, we have our butter, but most of all, we have each other."

The Olson family had a saying about eating together: "Where there is heart room, there is butt room."

There was a slogan a few years back: "Eat together eat better, eat better together." When we eat together, we get the nutrients from the food and the nutrients from the connections. There is such a wide variety of things to say and to do at mealtime, and every family has the opportunity to create different things. One thing is for sure—food is important to everyone and it provides many opportunities for making memories and connection.

It is by practicing these day-to-day rituals that we become the artist of every day, drawing picture memories that will last forever. In her book, *The Heart of a Family*, May Cox lists ten good things rituals do for children:
- Impact a sense of identity
- Provide comfort and security
- Help navigate change
- Teach values

- Cultivate knowledge of cultural or religious heritage
- Teach practical skills
- Solve problems
- Keep alive a sense of departed family members
- Create wonderful memories
- Generate joy

Books for Adults

Being Home, by Gunilla Norris

The meditations in this book show me the moment-to-moment awareness of paying attention to the ordinary events in my life.

The Heart of a Family: Searching America for New Traditions that Fulfill Us, by Meg Cox

Many good ideas on creating rituals that protect time as a family.

Books for Children

Hush Little Baby, by Sylvia Long

This is a rewritten version of an old lullaby. It reminds us to make connections with children rather than to buy something for children.

Query

Can you identify a time in your day that feeds your Spirit? Where are the stormy rumblings of transition in your day?

Quotes

"There are few hours in life more agreeable than the hour dedicated to the ceremony known as afternoon tea." Henry James

"A breakfast table looks different to someone who has milked cows, churned butter, slaughtered hogs, candled eggs, and dug potatoes."
Jackson Newell

"The birds perform a miracle every morning and we all ought to get up and listen to them!" Helen Simonson, in *Major Pettigrew's Last Stand*

"Meaning hides in repetition: we do this every day or every week because it matters. We are connected by this thing we do together. We matter to one another. In the tapestry of childhood, what stands out most is not the splashy, blow-out trip to Disneyland but the common threads that run throughout and repeat: the family dinners, nature walks, reading at bedtime, Saturday AM pancakes." Kim John Payne, in *Simplicity Parenting*

Poetry

"Community" by Starhawk
    Somewhere there are people
    to whom we can speak with passion
    without having the words catch in our throats.
    Somewhere a circle of hands will open to receive us,
    eyes will light up as we enter, voices will celebrate with us
    whenever we come into our own power.
    Community means strength that joins our strength
    to do the work that needs to be done.
    Arms to hold us when we falter.
    A circle of healing.
    A circle of friends
    Someplace where
    we can be free

"i thank you God for this most amazing" by E. E. Cummings

i thank You God for this most amazing
day: for the leaping greenly spirits of trees
and a blue true dream of sky; and for everything
which is natural which is infinite which is yes

(i who have died am alive again today,
and this is the sun's birthday; this is the birth
day of life and love and wings: and of the gay
great happening illimitably earth)

how should tasting touching hearing seeing
breathing any-lifted from the no
of all nothing-human merely being
doubt unimaginable You?

(now the ears of my ears awake and
now the eyes of my eyes are opened)

Song

"For Baby," by John Denver
I'll walk in the rain by your side I'll cling to the warmth of your tiny
hand
I'll do anything to help you understand
I'll love you more than anybody can
    And the wind will whisper your name to me
    Little birds will sing along in time
    The leaves will bow down when you walk by
    And morning bells will chime

I'll be there when you're feeling down
To kiss the tears if you cry
I'll share with you all the happiness I've found

A reflection of the love in your eyes
    And I'll sing you the songs of the rainbow
    Whisper all the joy that is mine
    the leaves will bow down when you walk by
    And morning bells will chime

Chapter 7
When Things Don't Go So Good, Don't Get Stuck—it's all about repair

A Chinese proverb, "Nobody's family can hang out the sign saying, 'nothing the matter here,'" states the truth I need to hear. I live in a less than perfect family with less than perfect parents, and I raise less than perfect children. I eventually learn that even families who look perfect go through difficult times. Given my desire for an efficient and peaceful household, it's easy to downplay the rough spots I encounter and just hope they will go away. I tell my children to "buck up," "be strong," "get over it," or "go play outdoors until you feel better," hoping my children will magically learn how to deal with conflict. What they learn is to stuff their feelings and ignore their problems.

Instead of banishing my children during times of stress or conflict, I can create rituals that remind me to pay attention to the negative feelings and conflicts within the family. Taking seriously the feelings of a child and the conflicts that emerge is a first step in teaching them that their feelings matter and that they are not alone in dealing with them.

An African tribe, the Babemba, have a ritual for a person who has created conflict in their tightly knit culture. The ritual goes like this: all work in the village halts when someone is having a problem. The people gather around the 'offender,' and one by one they begin to recite everything he has done right in his life: every good deed, thoughtful behavior, act of responsibility. These things have to be true, but the time-honored consequence of misbehavior is to appreciate that person back into the better part of himself. Rituals can help me get through rough spots by reminding me that I can forge connections rather than separateness during times of conflict; that within my family I do not have to allow angry feelings and conflicts to drive us apart. The transition focus of what is wrong with you to what is right with you is transformational.

Helping my child by asking, "What do you need?" and helping them find a better way to ask for what they need takes time and has long-term value.

Horace, in the book *Mean Soup* by Betsy Everett, had a very bad time at school. One day he forgot the answer to a question, and Zelda (his friend) gave him a love note, which he didn't appreciate at all, and the show-and-tell cow stepped on his foot. To make matters worse, his mother sent Miss Pearl to pick him up, and she drove so badly that she almost killed three poodles on the way home. As is often the way, his mother bore the brunt of his grumpiness. He hissed and growled when his mother asked how his day had been, and he threw a fall-on-the floor tantrum when she asked if he had thanked Miss Pearl for the ride home. Horace did not put words to his day, but his mom knew full well that it had not been a good day; she just didn't know *why*.

Like Horace, some children do not want to talk about their rough spots; it is usually their actions and mood that tell the story. We prod with questions and become frustrated when verbal answers are not forthcoming. So Horace's mom, being the wise woman she was, suggested they make a big pot of mean soup. They got the water boiling and threw in some salt. She screamed into the pot, then turned to Horace and said, "Your turn." They screamed and growled into the pot, they bared their teeth and stuck out their tongues, and banged the pot with a spoon. Horace's mother didn't need her ears to listen to Horace, she listened with her heart and created a ritual in which he could express his feelings, and the two of them could stay connected without having to talk about Horace's bad day when he wasn't ready to do so. Together they "stirred away a bad day."

The fact that Horace and his mother stirred the soup *together* is of no small significance. *Together* is the crucial word here. It would have been easier to say, "Horace, go to your room until you feel better," but if I consistently banish my child or ignore feelings during times of conflict, the seeds of isolation are planted. Noticing and acknowledging what a child experiences may seem like something we do automatically, but let's be honest, we can't really notice and acknowledge our child's feelings without some time and thought. Our ability to hang in there long enough to understand what's going on and develop a way through it requires that we be attentive to feelings. When the daunting demands of career and family totally focus my mind, I downshift my goals to "getting through" the day, thus tempting me to ignore or dismiss my child's emotional eruptions as no big deal. Stopping to address a six-year-old's stubbornness or a two-year-old's temper tantrum is more than inconvenient, it is downright impossible at times. Yet, taking seriously the feelings of a child and the conflicts that may ensue is worth every second of the time it takes because it is a first step in teaching children that their feelings matter and they are not alone in dealing with their rough spots.

It is no easier to address this in adult conversations. To really take time to listen to the feelings of another is the heart of communication. When feelings can be expressed, relief is in sight.

 ### Listening Later

There's not a parent alive who can't relate to the dilemma Joan faced one day. Tracy, Joan's six-year-old daughter, refused to get into the car seat as they were leaving to pick up Tracy's little brother at daycare. "Mom, I don't want to go," she whined. "Can't I stay home?"

"No, you can't, honey. There's no one home. Just jump in. We'll get John and be back in a minute."

Tracy stamped her foot and refused, and having learned the art of negotiation early, replied, "Then I'm going to buckle my own seatbelt."

Joan inwardly groaned since buckling the seatbelt was a new skill that could take an extra five minutes. She didn't have the extra time, and she didn't have the extra cash it would cost if she were late to pick up John. So without taking time to talk through the conflict, she picked up Tracy and buckled her into the seat.

Tracy settled down with only a whimper or two once she heard her mom say, "Let's do 'couch time' when Daddy gets home," because she knew she'd have her mother's full attention when they sat on a couch and talked, read a book, or just cuddled. Developing a ritual phrase such as "couch time," or "we'll talk about this later," or your family's own unique phrase such as, "we need popcorn time," when you don't have time to listen lets the child know that his or her feelings are important to you, and he or she can count on your attention later.

Phrases can be a manipulation instead of honest communication. Using the same phrase over and over is a ritual when it signals that I understand there is a problem and the child can count on my attention later; it becomes an empty habit if I don't follow through. Without follow-through, phrases become a bit of temporary appeasement that damages the trust I wish to build because my child learns that my words don't mean much. It is important for children to learn that their feelings cannot always be the top priority but that they are part of a family that listens to every person's needs in due time.

Rough-spot rituals don't keep children from having rough spots, but they can provide a tangible way to acknowledge the difficulty and move through it. Developing rituals to deal with rough spots can help me get from, "I don't want to talk to you," or "go to your room," to "let's figure out what the problem is and what we can do about it."

Going Down the Low Road

Children need you most when they are at their worst. Unfortunately, as a parent, this is often when I am at my worst. When I haven't taken time to explore all the ways I was dismissed as a child, I may find myself repeating messages I do not wish to pass on. Building nurturing relationships with children is not easy, and at times I "go down the low road" and end up needing to do repair work that starts with myself. By taking the time to understand my own childhood stories and how they actually shape the way I parent, I create a foundation for choosing intentional ways to help children through rough spots.

As a parent, I often find myself saying to my children the very thing my parents said to me. Some of the messages that pop into mind from childhood may well be nurturing and I can be grateful for those; others will not be. Daniel Siegel, a child psychiatrist who specializes in brain development, has researched the extent to which our own childhood experiences shape the way we parent. Drawing upon new findings in neurobiology and attachment research, he explains how interpersonal relationships, especially those we experience as children, directly impact the development of the brain. He points out that most parents want to be perfect, but most parents have times when they get too angry and "flip their lid." So when parents find themselves with their "bony finger in their child's face," it is time to stop, put our hands behind our backs, and take a time out. Then, when I've allowed time enough for the thinking part of my brain to return, I can do the repair work that is necessary to maintain secure attachments to my children. Repair rituals can provide a way to stop, repair, and reconnect.

Ever found yourself muttering, "Oh, I wish I hadn't gotten so mad," or "I sure wish I hadn't said that!" Welcome to the real world! Maya Angelou had it right when she said, "You did the best you could. When you knew better, you did better." Just remembering a phrase such as this can be a quiet, internal ritual that connects me to my better self—the one I just lost when I flew into a rage or made an angry comment that I later regretted.

Judy, my neighbor, shared a rough-spot ritual that worked for her family. She says, "When I did something with my children, Tova or Nathan, that I wished I hadn't done, I would ask if we could 'take two' of that scene. We would laugh, do it over, and I could respond in a way more fitting of a thoughtful parent. Tova and Nathan could also ask for a 'take two' of the scene.'" Another family, the Olsens, had an "erase it" phrase they used when communication was going south. Adding a phrase such as "take two" or "erase it" to my toolbox gives me a way to model for my children that it is okay to start over and try once again to communicate better. A phrase that immediately communicates a "whoops" moment can be more effective than just telling myself I am not going to make that mistake again. Creating a new interaction that communicates what I intend can provide a safety net that keeps anger and misunderstanding from mushrooming out of control.

I've Just Become My Father

But how about when we really blow it, when we "flip our lid" and a simple phrase is just not enough to reset and start over? One of my students, a father name Joe, found himself in such a spot one Saturday morning.

I picked up the phone that morning and heard Joe's frantic voice on other end of the line.

"I did it!" a distraught male voice came over the phone.

I had to take a minute to respond. First of all I had to place the voice. Joe hadn't even bothered to say his name. Then I had to pause and take a deep breath before answering because what I was remembering wasn't good. Joe's words were racing through my head—the words he had written the first day in class when I had asked everyone to write down their reasons for taking the class. Joe had written about the anger of his own father—the yelling, and the beatings, and how scared Joe had been of his dad when he was growing up. Joe had vowed that he was not going to pass that anger on.

"What did you do?" I finally managed to ask.

"I got so mad," Joe said in an anguished voice. Silence followed.

I waited. Dreading the next part, I asked, "Did you hit Kyle?"

"No. I got so mad I yelled at him and scared him half to death." Silence followed.

"I can't believe I yelled like that." Joe's voice broke, then he continued.

"I raised my fist, I've never done that before, and then I yelled that if he wasn't already sorry, I'd make him sorry. Same thing my dad yelled at me, and it was just over cleaning up his room. I just snapped!"

"Well, you didn't hit him," I said. "Where is he? Did he run away?"

"No, he's in his room sobbing."

We both knew that Joe's angry outburst could not be erased with a single phrase. That was why he was calling.

What could he do to mend what he had broken? Joe asked how he could regain that trust that Kyle had felt in him early on. Back then, his temper was not out of control. Joe was embarrassed by his anger—more than embarrassed—he was mortified. It had been hard enough for him to be honest about why he was in the parenting class, even harder to admit to me when we talked face to face that he had verbally abused Kyle.

When Kyle was ten, Joe was scared that he might haul off and hit his son, just like his father had done. He was angry with himself for not being able to control his temper, and uncomfortable and ashamed around Kyle. In the past, he hadn't even been able to apologize because he just wanted to get the angry episode behind him and move forward, vowing to never let it happen again. In spite of his love for Kyle and his ardent vows never to be like his dad, Joe was becoming exactly like him.

By the time he was thirty-eight, Joe was the vice president of the national midsize company where he worked. He had pretty much always accomplished what he set out to do. Joe was not used to failure. But this challenge—the challenge of uncontrolled anger toward his son—seemed beyond his control. And so here he was on a Saturday morning; his wife, Sandy, usually the buffer during tense times, was gone for the day, and he had turned to me for support. I remembered to tell Joe what someone once said to me, "Parenting is a great equalizer; I'm not as smug as I used to be." I also reminded Joe that he would learn the difference between shame and guilt. Shame never goes away, and we have to work hard at keeping it in check and not become the whole of who we are. Guilt is tied to an incident and can be changed.

Over the next few weeks with my urging and encouragement from Sandy, Joe began to face the fact that he couldn't meet this challenge by himself. He began to see a counselor.

At a reunion of their parenting class several years later, Joe told me, "You talked about rituals so much in our parenting class. I developed one that really helped me with my anger; in fact, it probably saved my relationship with Kyle.

"Remember that Saturday morning when I yelled at Kyle and got so scared I called you? You suggested that I find a friend I could call when I was angry and upset. At the time, I thought, *You gotta be crazy if you think I'll do that.* I did go to counseling and that was really important, but what helped me with Kyle was a ritual I developed with my friend Kevin. It took a couple of months before I was able to call him but I did."

"I called Kevin because I thought maybe he already knew the scoop with my dad. I was right. When I asked him if he remembered my dad, he said it would be hard to forget him. He had been at the house once when Dad hit me. That Saturday was the first time we had ever talked about what had happened. At the time, I just pretended it hadn't happened.

"At first I talked with Kevin almost every week whether I was angry or not. We started having breakfast on Saturday morning, and we'd talk about a lot more than just my anger, but I knew it wasn't something I had to keep from him. The ritual in all of this got started when I found myself getting angry with Kyle and immediately thinking, *I've got to talk to Kevin.* So I'd call Kevin. That was the ritual. It connected me to somebody who understood where I was coming from, and it connected me to the parent I wanted to be rather than the one who was out of control."

Ben Orki writes, "We are all wounded inside in some way or other. We all carry unhappiness within us for some reason or another. Which is why we need a little gentleness and healing from one another. Healing in word, healing beyond words. Like gestures. Warm gestures. Like friendship, which will always be like a mystery. Like a smile, which someone described as the 'shortest distance between two people.'"

Anticipating Rough Spots
Understanding Stages of Development

Understanding the stages of childhood can help me give guidance to my child by helping me understand what is possible for my child. My own clueless expectations are embarrassingly exposed when I find myself say-ing, "Stop acting like a little kid," when I am in fact talking to a five-year-old. Living with someone who acts like a nine-year-old one minute and a two-year-old the next is demanding. Once or twice a day I may be able to manage the roller coaster, but every hour, all day long, seven days a week? It's then I find myself saying phrases such as:

"It's not that big a deal."

"Get with the program. Let's move on."

"How dare you behave this way?"

"I'll show you who's boss!"

Understanding the developmental stages through which children progress can help me get through some of those "other" moments with a spirit of togetherness. Once again, remembering can bring authenticity to my interactions as I move through the stages of my childhood—this time with my children. Anna Quindlen recalls receiving a fortune cookie that said, "To remember is to understand." She goes on to say, "A judge remembers what it is like to be a lawyer. A good editor remembers being a writer. A good parent remembers what it is like to be a child."

Taking time to remember can help me identify with my children. That doesn't mean I indulge their feelings, but because my memories help me emotionally "get" what is going on, I'll be able to come up with state-ments that acknowledge their feelings with honest empathy. Once a child feels understood, they are likely to be ready to move beyond their feelings to next steps. Phrases such as:

"When I was little, life seemed overwhelming some times."

"It is hard to live in an adult world and not feel like you have any power."

"I can see how hard this is for you."

"It hurts when you don't get your own way."

Rough-spot rituals have two steps:

Step one: Remembering—this is internal and does not need to be shared, though at times my children felt quite comforted when I shared with them stories of my own childhood struggles.

Step two: Acknowledging my child's feelings—this is external. We come up with a thoughtful response that conveys understanding and empathy.

Feeling understood may be the only action necessary. Too often I try to fix it, and that can get in the way of listening and giving a thoughtful response. Now it is the child's work, to learn what to do about the emotions they feel.

A child's feelings can seem quite illogical to adult minds. A three-year-old could have just survived a tornado unfazed by the flying debris, but when she is served her favorite juice in a green cup instead of a purple cup, she completely falls apart. We try to use logic to calm the child—"It's your favorite juice and it's going to taste the same in the green cup." Or, when logic doesn't work, we go to commands: "Just drink the juice!"

To a three-year-old, the color of the cup can be as important as the juice. Knowing that a three-year-old's brain isn't capable of seeing the bigger picture and that a logical response isn't what a three-year-old can hear, a parent can help by stopping long enough to listen to what's behind the insistence on the purple cup. The "big picture" to the child is her feelings. Helping a children recognize their own feelings is a beginning step in helping them learn to navigate conflicts throughout their lives with friends, classmates, and coworkers, as well as family. Developing rituals to remind us that the need to pay attention to our child's negative feeling even when they don't make sense to us sets the stage for healthy conflict resolution throughout life.

Questions

Children ask about everything! Where does the snow come from? The clouds? Why do I have to bring my lunch to school? Why does Johnny get free school lunch? Why aren't we going on a vacation this year? Why aren't Ginny's parents married? Why do Grandma and Grandpa fight all the time? Why are Uncle Tim and Aunt Carolyn divorced? How come Mom lost her job? How come Maren has two dads and no mom? And then there are the really big questions—Where is God? Why can't we see her? Him? How come we pray before a meal? How come we don't pray before a meal like Annie does? Why does Uncle Brad have to fight in a war?

Children will ask a thousand questions during our lifetime. Questions begin before a child enters school and last until the teen years. Their questions charm, worry, frustrate, and perplex me; they make me feel important, scared, inadequate or frazzled, or all of those feelings at the same time. When I am aware and attentive to their questions, I can grow with them—understanding and accepting their needs as they change, and more likely respond with appropriate answers. If I truly hear them, I must listen "between the lines" and do the kind of high-powered listening that includes noticing the tone of voice, the body language, and the context. The answers I give them will help them interpret their world—who they are, who our family is, and how they fit into the world.

Sandy, the mother of four-year-old Laurie, six-year-old Mason, and nine-year old Justin, worked full time. She and her husband, Jason, shared parenting and household duties, but she still found herself exhausted and short with the children and their constant questions. When Justin was a toddler, she had been totally charmed by his questions; impressed, in fact, that he was such a curious child. Now she had three inquisitive children, and the constant barrage of questions irritated as often as delighted her.

One day when Justin had many questions about everything, from why his friend Tory was moving to why they had to go to Sunday school, Sandy totally lost it. She was worn down and she had tried to discourage him with short, quick answers, but when Justin was not to be dissuaded, something snapped and she responded by repeating, "Why do I have to go to Sunday school and Tory doesn't?" in a mocking voice. Justin looked shocked, then embarrassed, then left the room without a word.

Justin's exit prompted Sandy to realize that she had crossed the line, that the "thinking" part of her brain had stopped working. Justin, in all sincerity, was trying to understand his world and why it was different than Tory's. She realized he needed real answers—not the quick, factual retorts, and certainly not the mocking reply she had given when he asked about Sunday school. Why, she wondered, was she so impatient with Justin's questions? She didn't mind Laurie's. Laurie sometimes asked Sandy three or four times a day to tell her the "airplane story." Laurie had been adopted when she was two and she loved to hear her mom describe the airplane she came on, the attendant who carried her off the plane and handed her over into Sandy's arms, and how surprisingly small she had been. Because Sandy knew the story reassured Laurie, she didn't mind telling it three or four times a day. On the other hand, Justin's questions were becoming irritating. They required more of her. After all, how did she feel about divorce? What could she really say about Tory's parents divorcing—a question that would certainly come up if she told Justin that Tory was moving because his parents were divorcing. Why did they go to church? Even Mason's questions were beginning to tax her more than she liked to admit. He wondered where Grandpa had gone now that he had died, and if the guy who had broken into the house next door would be coming to their house. The world didn't make total sense to her, so how was she going to come up with answers that helped her children understand their world?

Children ask value-laden questions about topics that I may have pushed into the corners of my awareness not because they are unimportant to me, but precisely because they are. If I want to use my child's questions as an opportunity to pass on values, I need to be in an awakened state of mind. A state of mind in which I ask myself, "What makes me uncomfortable? What do I avoid answering? Am I really hearing my child's questions? If a question confuses me, do I search for clarity with my child?"

When Sandy brought her frustrations to parenting class one Monday evening, I shared a technique that had worked for me. When my children asked me a question that stumped me, I would tell myself, "This is the first time you've parented a five-year-old, so give yourself a break." Remembering who I was helped me remember that I was talking to a child. I was the adult. I was the one who had experience on my side, not the child. I gave myself permission to say, "I cannot answer that question right now but I will think about it and get back to you." This allowed me to be human and to have time to think and helped me change from you (the child) thinking to me (the adult) thinking.

Buying some time with statements such as these makes the interaction honest. When I am honest about my limitations, my children begin to understand that adults are human too. Children also begin to understand that Mom and Dad take their questions seriously.

Growing up is hard to do and childhood has its painful, embarrassing, and awkward moments. A bad report card, not having any friends, or losing a game because you struck out can feel as if you are the only one who has experienced these humiliating defeats.

Sylvia's son, Trevor, had a common junior high experience of being dumped by a girl. Trevor felt very sad, and his mom tried to say all the comforting things to try to help him feel better. None of them helped. On Saturday, he and his father always did the early morning paper route together. When they were done, his father said, "My brother and I had a thing we did when one of us got dumped; the other one had to take us out for breakfast. So how about we go out for breakfast?" Trevor's surprised response was, "You mean every time I get dumped we go out for breakfast?" A rough-spot ritual was in place. The "dumping breakfast" did not happen often, but when it did, Trevor was reminded that his father had been dumped too. Normalizing ("it happened to me") helps children get through awkward or embarrassing events.

Temperament

One day a couple lovingly planted a seed that they thought would grow to be the prized "Radiant Pink Carnation," a variety they both loved. They chose just the right location with morning sun and afternoon shade and were thrilled when the little seedlings emerged. With an abundance of optimism, they tilled the soil, added organic fertilizer, and watered every other day.

As the seedling grew, they noticed the leaves were a bit unusual. Concerned, they waited for the blossoms to appear and were disappointed to see they were not the shape or the shade of pink they were expecting. They became uncomfortable with their plant and avoided showing it to family and neighbors.

In private, the couple used pinking shears to make the leaves look more carnation like, and they carefully mixed the exact pink shade of paint to apply to each flower. The leaves began drooping and the entire plant seemed to lose its will to live.

The couple called in a horticulturist. She took one look at it and declared, "What have you done? This is one of the most beautiful and rarest roses imaginable, a Royal Crimson Perfectus, but something has kept it from developing properly!"

The couple looked at each other. Perhaps it wasn't too late. They threw their shears and brushes away. They realized that what they did to make the flower be exactly what they wanted and not realize the beauty it was becoming on its own.

This story, as told by Jane Stevesor, speaks to many of us about our misplaced efforts in parenting. We often assume our children will be like us, or just like their older brother or sister. But each baby is unique from the very beginning, and their temperament will be made up of a variety of traits such as the degree that they can concentrate, be active, adaptable, intense, or any other quality that makes up temperament.

I may resist accepting my child's temperament because it may not fit with my lifestyle, my expectations, or our family identity. After all, our family is outgoing and active, so how did we end up with Vince who is scared of new faces and fusses so easily? Or how did we end up with Annie who is so dramatic—she thrives on being the center of attention and loves to be the "director," and gets everyone involved in family play times and activities when we like peace and quiet, reading, and going with the flow.

I may find myself ignoring my child's temperament because I see it as a phase that I have to get through. Then, too, temperament is such a basic part of personhood, I may consider it unchangeable and therefore best ignored. I may describe my child's temperament as shy, stubborn, or rebellious, and while these descriptions might be accurate, they do nothing to help me deal with the difficulties these traits can engender. Being shy or stubborn or rebellious isn't easy for the child either. Ignoring temperament can add unnecessary difficulties because what the child naturally wants to do may be at odds with what parents or others expect. Over time they began to feel like failures. Major rough spots can develop when we try to change or modify our child's temperament, especially if the temperament is a challenging one.

My job as a parent is to help my children understand and manage their temperament.

Developing a family ritual or rituals to deal with rough spots can help me get from, "I don't want to talk to you," or "go to your room," to, "let's figure out what our problem is and what we can do about it." Because family problems and personalities are unique, so are the rituals that will effectively facilitate the necessary communication. In developing repair rituals, I will need to be attentive to each person's feelings and the idiosyncrasies of the situation. It won't happen overnight. These rituals will require heightened awareness, some time, and thought.

Developing your own rituals during times of conflict can:
- Alert everyone that there is a problem;
- Provide recognition, which brings validity to feelings;
- Provide a framework to count on;
- Assure everyone that "When we have a problem we deal with it, and we all deal with. Individual family members are not isolated by their problem."

Many of the techniques talked about in this chapter are about staying connected with children during times of conflict. However, all of the things mentioned in this chapter can also work with adults. We all have bad days and times when we say things that we regret. 'Starting over' is a universal tool for both children and adults. The need to be heard, the need to share feelings is also universal. American educator and author of

Seven Habits of Highly Effective People Stephen R. Covey wrote, "The biggest communication problem is we do not listen to understand, we listen to reply."

Books for Adults

Mind in the Making: The Seven Essential Life Skills Every Child Needs, by Ellen Galinsky
Insightful learning about what children really need.

Mindsight: the New Science Fiction of Personal Transformation, by Daniel Siegal
This is a must-read book about hope, and the positive influence hope can have in our lives.

My Grandfather's Blessings, by Rachel Naomi Remen, MD
This is a book with many lessons about healing when things don't go well!

Books for Children

Mean Soup, by Betsy Everitt
The story about a boy who has a bad day at school, and a mother's creation of a ritual to deal with his feelings about the day.

Fortunately, by Remy Charlip
An adventure of the ups and downs of life.

Go Away, Big Green Monster, by Ed Emberley
Overcoming the fear of monsters.

Pete's a Pizza, by William Steig
Humor helps a child deal with a disappointment.

King of the Playground, by Phyllis Reynolds Naylor
How to help a child handle a bully.

The Tree that Survived the Winter, by Mary Fahy
An encouraging book for all those who have overcome their own dark, cold, and lonely times.

Sun Bread, by Elisa Kleven
What to do on a dreary and gray winter day...make bread!

Thunder Cake, by Patricia Polacco
Making thunder cake helps a child face their own fears.

Query

Experience is a great teacher. What valuable lessons have I learned through getting through my own rough spots?

Where in my life am I called to be still and quiet enough to come to a clearer understanding of what to do? Until I have clear understanding of what *I* should do?

Identify a rough spot in your family.

Think about a time in your life when you learned a valuable lesson through experience.

Quote

"If you don't know where you're going, turn around and make sure you know where you're coming from." African saying

"Everything that happens to you is your teacher. The secret is to learn to sit at the feet of your own life and be taught by it." Polly Berends

"If in moving through your life, you find yourself lost, go back to the last place where you knew who you were, and start again from there." Bernice Johnson Reagon

"In order to arrive at what you do not know, you must go by a way which is the way of ignorance." T.S. Elliot

"If we hope to create a nonviolent world where respect and kindness replace fear and hatred, we must begin with how we treat each other at the beginning of life. For that is where our deepest patterns are set. From these roots grow fear and alienation—or love and trust." Suzanne Arms

"We do not grow absolutely, chronologically. We grow sometimes in one dimension, and not in another, unevenly. We grow partially. We are relative. We are mature in one realm, and childish in another." Anais Nin

A friend said, "A good title for a book: Things I Learned Again and Again and Again!"

"The road ahead may be veiled from sight but you must teach yourself to regard the unknown as friendly." Emmet Fox

"Good therapy helps. Good friends help. Pretending that we are doing better than we are doesn't. Shame doesn't. Being heard does." Anne Lamott

"Remember this too shall pass!" Ancient wisdom

"Hope is the feeling you have that the feeling you have isn't permanent." Jean Kerr

"In the middle of difficulty lies opportunity." Albert Einstein

"Even if the situation is hopeless, the mind is healthiest when it acts as if there is hope." Daniel Siegel

Poetry

"The Uses of Sorrow," by Mary Oliver, from *Thirst*
    Someone I loved once gave me
    a box full of darkness.

    It took me years to understand
    that this, too, was a gift.

"Chinese Restaurant" by David Shumate from *The Floating Bridge*
After an argument, my family always dined at the Chinese
restaurant. Something about the Orient washed the bitterness
away. Like a riverbank where you rest for awhile. The owner
bowed as we entered. The face of one who had seen too much.
A revolution. The torture of loved ones. Horrors he would never
reveal. His wife ushered us to our table. Her steps smaller than
ours. The younger daughter brought us tea. The older one took
our orders in perfect English. Each year her beauty was more
delicate than before. Sometimes we were the only customers
and they smiled from afar as we ate duck and shrimp with our
chopsticks. After dinner we sat in the comfort of their silence.
My brother told a joke. My mother folded a napkin into the shape
of a bird. My sister broke open our cookies and read our fortunes
aloud. As we left, my father always shook the old man's hand.

From Lao Tzu, in the *Tao Te Ching*
Do you have patience to wait

Till your mud settles and the water is clear?
    Can you remain unmoving
Till the right action arises by itself?

"Fire," by Judy Sorum, in *Brown From The Sea Accepts All Rivers and other Poems*
What makes a fire burn
a space between the logs,
a breathing space.
Too much of a good thing,
too many logs
packed in too tight
can douse the flames
almost as surely
as a pail of water would.

So building fires
requires attention
to the spaces in between,
as much as to the wood.

When we are able to build
open spaces
in the same way
we have learned
to pile on the logs,
then we can come to see how
it is fuel, and absence of the fuel
together, that makes fire possible.

We only need to lay a log
lightly from time to time. A fire

grows
simply because the space is there,
with openings
in which the flame
that knows just how it wants to burn
can find its way.

"Words," by Shinkichi Takahashi, in *Triumph of the Sparrow*
I don't take your words
merely as words.
Far from it.

I listen
to what makes you talk-
whatever that is-
and me listen.

From Rumi:
Out beyond ideas of wrong-doing and right-doing
There is a field
I'll meet you there.

When the soul lies down in that grass
The world is too full to talk about.

From Hafiz:
How
did the rose
ever open its heart

and give to this world
all its
beauty?

It felt the encouragement of light
against its
being.

Otherwise,
we all remain
too
frightened.

Song

"I Forgot to Remember to Forget," by Stan Kesler and Charlie
Feathers
    I forgot to remember to forget her.
    I can't seem to get her off my mind .
    I thought I'd never miss her.
    But I found out somehow
    I think about her almost all the time.
    The day she went away,
    I made myself a promise.
    That I'd soon forget we ever met.
    But something sure is wrong
    'Cause I'm so blue and lonely.
    I forgot to remember to forget.

"Bring Me A Rose" by Ernie Sheldon
Bring me a rose in the wintertime,
When they are hard to find.
Bring me a rose in the wintertime.
I've got roses on my mind;
For a rose is sweet at any time, and yet,
Bring me a rose in the wintertime.
How easy we forget.

Bring me a smile when you're far from home,
When they are hard to find.
Bring me a smile when you're far from home.
I've got smiling on my mind;
For a smile is sweet at any time, and yet,
Bring me a smile when you're far from home.
How easy we forget.

Bring me a kiss when my baby's grown
When they are hard to find.
Bring me a kiss when my baby's grown.
I've got kissing on my mind.
For a kiss is sweet at any time, and yet,
Bring me a kiss when my baby's grown.
How easy we forget.

Bring me love in the autumn years
When it is hard to find.
Bring me love in the autumn years.
I've got loving on my mind.
For love is sweet at any time, and yet,
Bring me love in the autumn years.
How easy we forget.

Bring me peace when there's talk of war,
When it is hard to find.
Bring me peace when there's talk of war,
For peace is on my mind;
For peace is sweet at any time, and yet,
Bring me peace when there's talk of war.
How easy we forget

Chapter 8
Some Favorite Resources

Gift Giving

Adults
- This is an idea for an adult who does not need anything specific but whom we want to let know how much we love them. Give a gift of five postcards addressed to you. On the backside of the postcard, draw or cut out picture of things you'd be good at making and that you know they like. Then, during the year, when the person wants to order that something, they will send you the postcard of their choice, and that is what you will make for them. You send back the ordered goodie. It is a great homemade way to say, "I love you!"

- Phone box for parents or grandparents. My worst time with my own children usually occurred when I was on the phone. They always seemed to have needs just as a phone call came. I was relieved to hear an idea from a neighbor who had raised six children. She had developed a phone box that was used exclusively while she was on the phone. It contained all kinds of interesting objects that changed from time to time. The objects occupied children's interest during phone time and when the call was done, the box went away. It saved me many potentially frustrating phone calls.

- A prediction jar for New Year's celebrations. Every member of the family writes a prediction for the coming year and sticks them into the prediction jar. The following New Year begins by reading the predictions written for last year and everyone rewriting new ones.

Children
- The best gift I gave my son one Christmas was a box of oranges, a knife, a cutting board, orange juice squeezer, and some little

glasses. He had fun making drinks for his friends as well as everyone who came to visit.

- Most gifts for children are bought at thrift stores and hardware stores. We had the best dress-up clothes in town. Lots of variety and fun extensions to play with, such as pails, flashlights, nails, and tubes of all kinds. It did not take long before neighbor children knew they could come to our house for ideas for costumes.
- A tree stump (felt the bottom). My Uncle Andrew always had a tree stump in the hallway leading to the kitchen. It was my children's favorite thing when we visited. I made one for my own kitchen. Children would come home from school and pound nails into the tree stump. It provided something for children to do when they needed a transition time between school and home as well as a good diversion when I was making meals.
- Just-a-minute-box: This idea came to me one day with two small children in tow and too many errands. I realized how many times that day I had said, "wait one minute more." The idea for a just-a-minute box came that day. I used a plastic fishing tackle box and filled it with good waiting stuff like pencils and pens and colors and paper and a few wind up small toys and just fun things to do. Much like the phone box. It was magical for in the car or restaurant or doctor offices—anywhere waiting happened, the box came with us.
- Infant pillow: How many times have you had near accidents driving while trying to retrieve a small treasure for a crying infant or toddler? My mother-in-law, Jeanne, solved this problem with a self-contained entertainment center. She would sew enticing objects like keys, measuring spoons, and other fun stuff onto a square pillow. So when it was dropped in the car it was easily retrievable.
- A family service bell, so when someone is sick in the family, they can have the bell by their bed and ring it for service. A small comfort when you are sick and can't go out to play.

Birthday

- A wish pillow is a small pillow with a pocket sewed on it. Family and friends write birthday wishes on sheets of paper that are tucked into the pocket. The birthday person gets to sleep with the pillow and begins their day reading each person's wish for the coming year. Could also be used for someone who is sick...send them a pillow with a pocketful of well wishes. It can also be used for a wedding shower or a baby shower.
- Hundred penny boxes are fun and easy to do. Give a penny and a picture from that year and write something you remember about the person from that year.
- Build a library for a child and give a book each year and write some kind of message that might include a memory or picture from the year.
- Flash paper is an exciting addition to a birthday or a New Year's celebration. Flash paper is found in most magic stores and when ignited by an open flame like a candle, the paper burns quickly and completely with no ash or smoke. Write a wish and light it... and send the wish out to the universe! Flash paper sparkles up many an occasion.

Grand Parenting: Building Relationships Over Time

I am not a grandparent, so I asked my friend Alice Evans (a grandparent I greatly admire) to share what she does. The following is what she wrote (the "I" in the following is Alice):

Becoming a grandparent is an exciting event, but it also presents the challenge of how to connect with these new people, and how to be a presence in their lives whether they live near or far. Distance makes things harder, but not impossible. Grandparents have to figure out how to make these connections happen. Setting up repetitive events or rituals can help. This writing shares my process.

Grandma Alice's Time: Connecting through Sharing Interests and Fun Times

Having fun together is the most obvious response to how to connect, but with boys and girls of different ages what to do is the question. My grandchildren came in a bunch, seven boys and girls in seven years! My first grandma times started with babysitting. This time alone with the children helped me get to know their personalities and temperaments. Spending time at my house also gave my adult children a parenting time out. A win-win for all. It seems that in our busy families the gift we most need from each other is personal attention and time. So I began to invent special times (rituals) to be together with my grandchildren (preferably on a one-on-one basis).

Beginning about age two, I began taking the children to Target to Christmas shop. They were each given a small amount of money, and with much excitement, they picked out special presents for their mom and dad. Together, we wrapped the gifts and hid them to keep secret until Christmas (which usually they could not do). My adult children loved their choices from Barbie watches, gaudy fishing flies, and superhero pencils. They delighted in the lovingly selected gifts and the joy the children expressed in giving (an important value).

I also began a new yearly ritual for my Christmas giving, the Grandma Coupon. My Christmas gift would be a book and a coupon for a "Special Time with Grandma" (good for one year). The children were to decide what that special time would be. (Their parents helped with ideas for fun). The trick was defining what is special. One grandchild may only want a trip out for ice cream or an overnight sleepover at my house playing Bingo. Others may want me to ride with them on scary carnival rides. As the grandchildren have grown and developed special interests, activities and events have also changed. Middle-school garage-rock-band concerts and movies with lots of monsters and car crashes. Some chosen events have been hard for me to get excited about; however, the key to a kid's special event is a willingness to change and be creative in the spending of time together. It is important to remember the goal is connecting. Although spending time together usually does not involve a great deal of expense, (movie tickets, popcorn) I do set a dollar limit for the coupons, keeping things equal and simple. The event usually includes eating at a place of their choice and a visit.

Once the grandchildren turn eighteen and graduate from high school, the Christmas ritual changes to a money gift, book and coupon for coffee, lunch etc., for little catch-up visits. I have done this Grandma Coupon for over twenty years now and it has enriched my life greatly. I have been able to be a part of my grandchildren's growing up, to share their interests and disappointments, and to know each one as an individual. Over the years, this Christmas coupon ritual has produced many fun times and precious memories for myself and my family.

Celebrating Important Events with Affirmations and Past and Present-Time Gifts

Celebrating special events with my grandchildren has evolved into a personal ritual for me. I write a personal letter sharing my thoughts and affirmations about this time in their lives, and I also give them a past and present gift. The "past" gift is a family artifact that I thought they would enjoy having (Grandpa's marble collection) along with a bit of family history about that individual. The "now" gift celebrates the present with money tucked in for fun and a special treat.

As the family historian, I have also written ancestor stories for the children to take along on special trips. The trick is to write family history in an interesting, age-appropriate manner. For example, when a teenaged grandson wanted to hike in the Wyoming mountains, I sent stories about on his great-grandparents' pioneer days in that area and their run-in with outlaws, the Sheep and Cattle wars, etc. Again, when two elementary age grandchildren took a trip to my West coast hometown without me, I sent pictures and stories of my growing up, including stories of an organ grinder and monkey, fights with my sister, and embarrassing elementary school experiences. The whole family has seemed to enjoy these little bits of history.

Building relationships over time with grandchildren is an ongoing creative process of special interactions and activities. I have shared some of my ideas, but each grand-parenting experience is unique and requires developing one's own connecting rituals and celebrations. However, in the end, connecting and being present with others is mostly a matter of paying individual attention to those we love and being there (in person or Spirit) for events large and small. Being a grandparent brings many gifts, not the least is joy and hope for the future. It is wonderful to be part of these enriching relationships."

The resources in this chapter may or may not fit for your family. I offer them simply as ideas. Take what you like and ignore the rest. Let the spirit of experimentation, without any judgment, and your own heart be your best guides.

Post Script

As I wrote that final paragraph, there occurred yet another school shooting, this time close to home. We live in a time when many people feel disconnected and isolated. I do not believe that ritual is a cure-all, but I *do* believe that there would be fewer of these heinous acts if individuals felt a connection with others, and found a place of belonging. Belonging is the very basic curriculum of life. It should be the very basic curriculum in our schools also. The most important thing we can do is to protect time, so that connecting and belonging can begin to happen in our families and our communities. I believe that if we begin to take time to tend hearts, we will strengthen ourselves and our world.

THE HEART
OF
EDUCATION
IS
EDUCATION
OF
THE HEART!
Anonymous

Acknowledgments
People Who Have
Tended My Heart

There is a saying, "If you see a turtle on the top of a fence post, you know it has had help getting there." I have had many moments in my life where I realized I was on top of a fence post and had support to get there. This book has taught me just how much patience and hard work goes into writing. In fact, I have learned as much by writing as I have by all my years of reading. There have been many kind souls helping me, guiding me, and tending my heart.

My first thanks goes out to Audrey Rogness. She has taught me so much about friendship and writing. This started out in fact as a joint project, and it has ended up with me finishing solo.

My daughter, Kate, has been my confidante and rewriting consultant. Her confidence in me has sustained me through many hand-wringing moments. Her best line to me, "It goes dead here, Mom."

To my friend Winky who has helped in so many ways. Her advice, "Always end each day knowing what you are going to write the next…even if it is midsentence, that's what Hemingway always did." She and her husband Peter have supported me in ways that allowed me to keep on keeping on!

To parents in my co-op classes at Seattle Central Community College and Skagit Valley College. Thanks for their honest sharing of stories. Family life is a challenge and we realize that challenge in the midst of daily being a parent.

To Alice Evans, who gave clarity to the notion that this book should not make the reader feel guilty. Her sharing is a gift and gives so many clues about what it means to stay connected over time with grandchildren. Thanks for her contribution about her experience of grand-parenting.

To Morgan Sharp for the photo of the candles on the front cover.

To Judy Endenstrom and Kristin Peterson for the art work on the back cover.

To Savannah Ray for the inside illustrations.

To Roz Ray who helped me through the editing process.

The neighbors in my Whidbey Island community that patiently asked, "Is it done yet?" Especially Nancy and Sue, who were my constant computer fixers. And to Chris who helped me out with muscle support for yard work and house repairs.

The community college colleagues who helped me formulate early pieces.

The new readers in Seattle: Judy, Kristin, Chris, Maralyn, Mary, and Connie. They believed that this book could actually be finished.

To Jean Giono who wrote the book, *The Man Who Planted Trees*. It took twenty-three years to write, and in the end it was seven typed pages. It is an inspirational book about perseverance, hope, and humility—all the qualities I needed for finishing my own book.

My Quaker friends who joyfully profess an experience-based faith. They express that faith through what they do, rather than what they say.

Partners, allies, confidants, and many many kind souls who gave me direction, nourishment, inspiration, and coffee.

And finally to my own parents, Ordin and Alvera. Their faithfulness to practice ritual out of their own values in every season of the year contributed to my rich memory bank.

And finally to Smokie the Cat, who ran by my house skinny as a rail and after five months of feeding let me pet her. She provided breaks during my writing because I could hear her on my front steps call for some attention. And thanks to my indoor cat Tess, who sat in my lap as I worked at my computer.

Arthur Miller said, "Like every writer, I am asked where my work originates, and if I knew I would go there more often." I go to all the above mentioned people and animals often and am filled with such gratitude for all the ways they have helped me get to finally type. The End!

Bibliography

Books

Bayor, Byrd. *The Way to Begin the Day* (Aladdin: 1986)

Beeler, Selby B., G. Brian Karas (illustrator), *Throw Your Tooth on the Roof (Tooth Traditions from Around the World)* (HMH Books for Young Readers: 2001)

Boynton, Sandra, *Yay, You!* (Little Simon: 2001)

Bridges, William, *Managing Transitions: Making the Most of Change* (Da Capo Lifelong Books: 2009)

Carle, Eric, *"Slowly, Slowly, Slowly," said the Sloth* (Puffin: 2007)

Charlip, Remy, *Fortunately* (Aladdin: 1993)

Connolly, Patrick, *Love Dad* (Andrews McMeel Pub: 1985)

Coppock Stacheli, Jean, and Joe Robinson, *Unplug the Christmas Machine: A Complete Guide to Putting Love and Joy Back Into the Season* (William Morrow: 1991)

Covey, Stephen R., *Seven Habits of Highly Effective People: Powerful Lessons in Personal Change* (DC Books: 2005)

Cox, Meg, *The Heart of a Family: Searching America for New Traditions That Fulfill Us* (Random House: 1998)

Davies, Valentine, *Miracle on 34th Street* (Amereon Ltd: 1984)

Doherty, William J., Ph.D., Barbara Carlson, *Putting Family First: Successful Strategies for Reclaiming Family Life in a Hurry-Up World* (Macmillan: 2002)

Dostoevsky, Fyodor, *The Brothers Karamozov*, David McDuff, Trans., (Penguin Classics: 2003)

Elkind, David, *The Hurried Child: Growing Up Too Fast Too Soon* (Da Capo Press: 1981)

Emberley, Ed, *Go Away, Big Green Monster* (Little, Brown and Company: 1992)

Everett, Betsy, *Mean Soup* (HMH Books for Young Readers: 1995)

Fahy, Mary, Emil Antonucci (illustrator), *The Tree that Survived the Winter* (Paulist Press: 2001)

Fulghum, Robert, *From Beginning to End: The Rituals of Our Lives* (Ballantine Books: 1995)

Galinsky, Ellen, *Mind in the Making: The Seven Essential Life Skills Every Child Needs* (Harper Collins: 2010)

Hummel, Charles, *Tyranny of the Urgent* (Inter-Varsity Christian Fellowship of the United States of America: 1967)

Igus, Toyomi, *Two Mrs. Gibsons* (Children's Book Press: 2001)

Imber-Black, Evan, Ph.D., and Janine Roberts, Ed.D., *Rituals for Our Times: Celebrating, Healing, and Changing Our Lives and Our Relationships* (Rowman & Littlefield Publishers, Inc.: 1992)

Ingpen, Roberth, and Bryan Mellonie, *Lifetimes: The Beautiful Way to Explain Death to Children* (Bantam: 1983)

Kleven, Elisa, *Sun Bread* (Puffin: 2004)

Kubler-Ross, Elizabeth, *On Death and Dying* (Scribner: 1997)

Lao Tzu, *Tao Te Ching*

Lindbergh, Anne Morrow, *Gift from the Sea: An Answer to the Conflicts in Our Lives* Pantheon Books: 1991)

Long, Sylvia, *Hush Little Baby* (Chronicle Books: 2002)

Lovell, Patty, David Catrow (illustrator) *Stand Tall, Molly Lou Melon* (G.P. Putnam's Sons: 2001)

Luskin, Fred, Ph.D., *Forgive for Good: A Proven Prescription for Health and Happiness* (Harper Collins Publishers: 2002)

MacLachlan, Patricia, Michael Wimmer (illustrator), *All the Places to Love* (HarperCollins: 1994)

Barry Moser (illustrator), *What You Know First* (HarperCollins: 1998)

Mathis, Sharon Bell, *The Hundred Penny Box* (Puffin: 2006)

Muller, Wayne, *Sabbath: Finding Rest, Renewal, and Delight in Our Busy Lives* (Bantam: 2000)

Muth, Jon. J., *Three Questions, Based on a Story by Leo Tolstoy* (Scholastic Press: 2002)

Naylor, Phyllis Reynolds, Nola Langner Malone (illustrator), *King of the Playground* (Atheneum Books for Young Readers: 1994)

Nepo, Mark, *The Book of Awakening: Having the Life You Want by Being Present in the Life You Have* (Conari Press: 2000)

Norris, Gunilla, Greta D. Sibley (photographer), *Being Home* (Random House LLC: 2012)

Nouwen, Henri J.M., *Reaching Out: The Three Movements of the Spiritual Life* (Image: 1986)

Bass, Dorothy C., ed., *Practicing Our Faith* (Jossey-Bass: 2010)

Pipher, Mary, Ph.D., *In the Shelter of Each Other* (Riverhead Trade: 2008)

Polacco, Patricia, *Thunder Cake* (Puffin: 1997)

Remen, Rachel Naomi, M.D., *My Grandfather's Blessings: Stories of Strength, Refuge, and Belonging* (Riverhead Trade: 2001)

Rogers, Fred and Barry Head, *Mr. Rogers Talks With Parents* (Hal Leonard Corporation: 1993)

Steig, William, *Pete's a Pizza* (HarperFestival: 2003)

Stevens, Barry, *Don't Push the River* (Real People Press: 1970)

Tillman, Nancy, *Wherever You Are: My Love Will Find You* (Feiwel & Friends: 2012)

Tolstoy, Leo, *What Men Live By and Other Tales* (Nabu Press: 2010)

de Vinck, Christopher, *Only the Heart Knows How to Find Them: Precious Memories for a Faithless Time* (Penguin Books: 1993)

Walton, Charlie, *When There are No Words: Finding Your Way to Cope with Loss and Grief* (Pathfinder Publishing: 1999)

White, E.B., *Charlotte's Web* (HarperCollins: 2012)

Willard, Nancy, Richard Jesse Watson (illustrator), *The High Rise Glorious Skittle Skat Roarious Sky Pie Angel Food Cake* (Voyager Books: 1996)

Wolin, Steven and Sybil, *The Resilient Self* (Villard: 1993)

Wood, Douglas, *The Secret of Saying Thanks* (Simon & Schuster Books for Young Readers: 2005)

Film

Babette's Feast (1987)

Poetry

Berry, Wendell, "Closing the Circle."

e.e. cummings, "i thank you God for this most amazing."

Edenstrom, Judy, "Artists."

Hafiz, *The Gift: Poems by Hafiz, the Great Sufi Master,* trans. Daniel Ladinsky.

Harcourt, Jan, "No Need to Mourn."

Horne, Frank, "Kid Stuff." (1942)

Longfellow, Henry Wadsworth, *Holidays.*

Lyon, George Ella. *Reading, Writing and Rising Up.*

Merriman, Eve. "A Lazy Thought."

Oliver, Mary, *Thirst*, (Beacon Press 2006)

Rumi, *Essential Rumi,* trans. Coleman Barks.

Shumate, David, *The Floating Bridge,* (University of Pittsburgh Press 2008)

Sorum, Judy, *The Sea Accepts All Rivers and Other Poems,* (2000)

Stafford, William, *The Way It Is: New and Selected Poems.* (Graywolf Press, 1998)

Starhawk, "Community."

Tai, Eve M., "Generations (for the forests of Ellsworth Creek)."

Takahashi, Shinkichi, *Triumph of the Sparrow*, (1986)

Viorst, Judith, *Necessary Losses.*

Songs

Leonard Cohen, "Anthem," on *The Future*

John Denver, "For Baby," on *Rocky Mountain High*

Charlie Feathers and Stan Kesler, "I Forgot to Remember to Forget," on *Wild Side of Lie*

Isaye Barnwell, "Wanting Memories," on *Sweet Honey in the Rock*

Ronnie Gilbert, "There was Music"

Sally Rogers, "Circle of the Sun," on *The Unclaimed Pint/In the Circle of the Sun*

Ernie Sheldon, "Bring Me A Rose"

Paul Simon, "The 59th Street Bridge Song (Feelin' Groovy)," in *Parsley, Sage, Rosemary and Thyme*

The Supremes, "Stop! In the Name of Love!," in *More Hits by The Supremes*

Quotes

A friend said, "A good title for a book: Things I Learned Again and Again and Again!"

African saying, "If you don't know where you're going, turn around and make sure you know where you're coming from."

Ancient Wisdom, "Remember this too shall pass!"

Suzanne Arms, "If we hope to create a nonviolent world where respect and kindness replace fear and hatred, we must begin with how we treat each other at the beginning of life. For that is where our deepest patterns are set. From these roots grow fear and alienation—or love and trust."

Bepko and Krestan, "Celebrations make beginnings, endings, comings and goings, without it we feel emptiness and alienation in our lives."

Polly Berends, "Everything that happens to you is your teacher. The secret is to learn to sit at the feet of your own life and be taught by it."

William Bridges, "It isn't the changes that do you in, it's the transitions."

Herb Brokering, "Childhood feelings are the oldest footnotes in you. The child in me is the foundation of my life. I go there in all my writings. It's about imaging, imagination. Two days before Christmas my brother died. So

Christmas got all mixed up with Sunday, Easter, Good Friday and all the clocks broke in my mind. All the Seasonal boundaries broke."

Elder Cherokee Man, "A fight is going on inside me...it is a terrible fight, and it is between two wolves. One wolf represents fear, anger, greed, arrogance, resentment, pride, and superiority. The other wolf stands for peace, hope, humility, kindness, benevolence, generosity, and compassion. This same fight is going on inside of you and every other person too." [His grandchildren] thought about it for a minute and then one child asked his grandfather, "Which wolf will win?" The old Cherokee simply replied, "The one I feed."

Cheyenne saying, "Our first teacher is our own heart."

A Chinese proverb, "Nobody's family can hang out the sign saying, 'nothing the matter here.'"

Albert Einstein, "In the middle of difficulty lies opportunity."

T.S. Elliot, "In order to arrive at what you do not know, you must go by a way which is the way of ignorance."

Emmet Fox, "The road ahead may be veiled from sight but you must teach yourself to regard the unknown as friendly."

Mohandas Gandhi, "There is more to life than increasing its speed."

Jan Howard, "Call it a clan, call it a network, call it a tribe, call it a family. Whatever you call it, whoever you are, you need one."

Jesse Jackson, "Your children need your presence not your presents."

Ruby Jackson, "The Lord made us family. Miles can't keep us apart. Time can't make us forget. Troubles can't put away our hope and our pride. We go on praying. We go on dreaming. We go on living with peace and courage in our hearts. And we make this world a better home for all generations to come."

Henry James, "There are few hours in life more agreeable than the hour dedicated to the ceremony known as afternoon tea."

Samuel Johnson, "To be happy at home is the ultimate result of all ambition."

Jean Kerr, "Hope is the feeling you have that the feeling you have isn't permanent."

Ann Lamott, "Good therapy helps. Good friends help. Pretending that we are doing better than we are doesn't. Shame doesn't. Being heard does." (in *Stitches: A Handbook on Meaning, Hope and Repair*)

Ann Morrow Lindbergh, "Perhaps this is the most important thing for me to take back from beach-living; simply the memory that each cycle of the tide is valid, each cycle of the wave is valid, each cycle of a relationship is valid." (in *Gift from the Sea*)

W. Somerset Maugham, "Tradition is a guide not a jailer."

Gertrude Nelson, "Rituals draw a circle around a place or event so that we can be more fully awake to the magnitude of the moment." (in *To Dance With God*)

Mark Nepo, "If you truly hold a stone, you can feel the mountain it came from." (in *Seven Thousand Ways to Listen: Staying Close to What is Sacred*)

Jackson Newell, "A breakfast table looks different to someone who has milked cows, churned butter, slaughtered hogs, candled eggs, and dug potatoes." (in *The Geography of Childhood: Why Children Need Wild Places*)

Reinhold Niebuhr, "Nothing we do, however virtuous, can be accomplished alone; therefore, we are saved by love."

Anais Nin, "We do not grow absolutely, chronologically. We grow sometimes in one dimension, and not in another, unevenly. We grow partially. We are relative. We are mature in one realm, and childish in another."

--"The heart has its own memory. Each friend represents a world in us and it is by this world that a new world is born."

Georgia O'Keeffe, "To see takes time."

Ben Orki, "We are all wounded inside in some way or other. We all carry unhappiness within us for some reason or another. Which is why we need a little gentleness and healing from one another. Healing in word, healing beyond words. Like gestures. Warm gestures. Like friendship, which will always be like a mystery. Like a smile, which someone described as the 'shortest distance between two people.'"

Kim John Payne, "We are connected by the things we do together. There is regularity, a consistency to what we do as a family. Quite simply: rhythm and ritual are what we aim for; predictability may be what we can achieve."

"Meaning hides in repetition: we do this every day or every week because it matters. We are connected by this thing we do together. We matter to one another. In the tapestry of childhood, what stands out most is not the splashy, blow-out trip to Disneyland but the common threads that run throughout and repeat: the family dinners, nature walks, reading at bedtime, Saturday AM pancakes." (in *Simplicity Parenting*)

Anna Quindlen, "A judge remembers what it is like to be a lawyer. A good editor remembers being a writer. A good parent remembers what it is like to be a child."

Bernice Johnson Reagon, "If in moving through your life, you find yourself lost, go back to the last place where you knew who you were, and start again from there."

Rainier Maria Rilke, "Have patience with everything unresolved in your heart, and try to love the questions themselves as if they were locked rooms or books written in a very foreign language." (in *Reaching Out,* Henri J.M. Nouwen)

Dr. Janine Roberts, "People are returning to family rituals because the world is losing a sense of what's important, offering instead shallow beliefs and sound-bite values. Family rituals help people affirm what their beliefs really are." (in *Rituals for Our Times*)

Nancy Rubin, "Rituals are part of the glue that holds a family together, a way of communicating intimacy and love and security. They define us as a culture, as a family, as individuals, they change as we change." (in *The Book of Traditions*)

John Ruskin, "We are not sent into this world to do anything into which we cannot put our heart."

Socrates, "Beware of the barrenness of a busy life."

Helen Simonson, "The birds perform a miracle every morning and we all ought to get up and listen to them!" (in *Major Pettigrew's Last Stand*)

Lily Tomlin, "For fast-acting relief, try slowing down."

About The Author

Karin Elizabeth Watson has had a long career in education. Her professional qualifications include a BA in Sociology from Augsburg College in Minneapolis, Minnesota; certification in Early Childhood Education from the University of Minnesota; and American Montessori certification. She has forty-five years of teaching experience in community colleges in Seattle and Skagit Valley, Washington and Minnesota. She also worked for five years developing parent education programs at the Island County Health Department in the state of Washington.

Inspired by her own family experiences, as well as by encouragement from her parent education colleagues and families in her classes, Watson authored the book *Heart Tending.*

The author was married for twenty-seven years and has two grown children, whom she credits as her best guides and teachers.